Cambridge Elements

Elements in Politics and Communication
edited by
Stuart Soroka
University of California, Los Angeles

NEWS USE, POLITICAL KNOWLEDGE, AND MISPERCEPTIONS IN 18 COUNTRIES ACROSS THE GLOBAL NORTH

Peter Van Aelst
University of Antwerp

Luisa Gehle
Johannes Gutenberg University Mainz

Christian Schemer
Johannes Gutenberg University Mainz

Jesper Strömbäck
University of Gothenburg

Alon Zoizner
University of Haifa

Shaftesbury Road, Cambridge CB2 8EA, United Kingdom

One Liberty Plaza, 20th Floor, New York, NY 10006, USA

477 Williamstown Road, Port Melbourne, VIC 3207, Australia

314–321, 3rd Floor, Plot 3, Splendor Forum, Jasola District Centre, New Delhi – 110025, India

Cambridge University Press is part of Cambridge University Press & Assessment, a department of the University of Cambridge.

We share the University's mission to contribute to society through the pursuit of education, learning and research at the highest international levels of excellence.

www.cambridge.org
Information on this title: www.cambridge.org/9781009632447
DOI: 10.1017/9781009632430

© Peter Van Aelst, Luisa Gehle, Christian Schemer, Jesper Strömbäck, and Alon Zoizner 2026

This publication is in copyright. Subject to statutory exception and to the provisions of relevant collective licensing agreements, no reproduction of any part may take place without the written permission of Cambridge University Press & Assessment.

When citing this work, please include a reference to the DOI 10.1017/9781009632430

First published 2026

A catalogue record for this publication is available from the British Library

A Cataloging-in-Publication data record for this Element is available from the Library of Congress

ISBN 978-1-009-63244-7 Hardback
ISBN 978-1-009-63247-8 Paperback
ISSN 2633-9897 (online)
ISSN 2633-9889 (print)

Additional resources for this publication at www.cambridge.org/9781009632447.

Cambridge University Press & Assessment has no responsibility for the persistence or accuracy of URLs for external or third-party internet websites referred to in this publication and does not guarantee that any content on such websites is, or will remain, accurate or appropriate.

For EU product safety concerns, contact us at Calle de José Abascal, 56, 1°, 28003 Madrid, Spain, or email eugpsr@cambridge.org

News Use, Political Knowledge, and Misperceptions in 18 Countries across the Global North

Elements in Politics and Communication

DOI: 10.1017/9781009632430
First published online: February 2026

Peter Van Aelst
University of Antwerp

Luisa Gehle
Johannes Gutenberg University Mainz

Christian Schemer
Johannes Gutenberg University Mainz

Jesper Strömbäck
University of Gothenburg

Alon Zoizner
University of Haifa

Author for correspondence: Peter Van Aelst, peter.vanaelst@uantwerpen.be

Abstract: The established idea that people learn about politics and relevant societal issues via the news media can be put into question because of a "twin challenge of increased media choice." First, there is a growing number of people who choose to avoid most news which leaves them uninformed about what is happening in politics and society. Second, people may form their beliefs based on false and misleading information, leading them to become misinformed about current political issues. This Element investigated both challenges based on data from a large comparative survey in eighteen Western countries. Consistent with the existing literature, the results largely confirm the added value of staying informed through using traditional news media, the public broadcaster in particular. In contrast, consuming news from newer media sources such as social media and messaging apps is typically associated across countries with less knowledge and more misperceptions about political matters.

Keywords: political knowledge, news media, public broadcaster, misbeliefs, social media

© Peter Van Aelst, Luisa Gehle, Christian Schemer, Jesper Strömbäck, and Alon Zoizner 2026

ISBNs: 9781009632447 (HB), 9781009632478 (PB), 9781009632430 (OC)
ISSNs: 2633-9897 (online), 2633-9889 (print)

Contents

1 Introduction: Political Knowledge Challenged by the High-Choice Media Environment … 1

2 Methodology and Data … 7

3 News Use and Political Knowledge … 22

4 News Use and Misperceptions … 29

5 The Importance of Different Types of TV News and Newspapers … 36

6 Variations across Countries … 50

7 Discussion … 74

References … 82

1 Introduction: Political Knowledge Challenged by the High-Choice Media Environment

In the contemporary media environment, it is hard to imagine a time when news was a scarcity, only delivered a few times a day at fixed times, almost exclusively consumed at home in the living room or at the kitchen table, and when most people were exposed to news that was highly similar regardless of which TV-news show or newspaper people in a certain geographic area were taking part in. It is almost as hard as it is to imagine that phones were something exclusively used to call people. Still, it was only about thirty years ago.

Since then, the Internet and digitalization have radically transformed media environments across the world. Low-choice media environments have been replaced by high-choice media environments, offering a greater abundance of news and information than ever before, where people can access information from virtually anywhere at times and places of their own choosing (Chadwick, 2013; Prior, 2007; Van Aelst et al., 2017).

As part of this process, the role of traditional news media has been severely challenged and weakened. Importantly, they have lost much of their original function as gatekeepers to the broader public sphere (Bruns, 2018; Shoemaker & Vos, 2009; Strömbäck, Boomgaarden et al., 2022). Although traditional news media are still highly important as producers and sources of news about politics and society (Castro et al., 2022; Newman et al., 2023), and are still tasked with the key function of verifying the accuracy and truthfulness of information before publishing it (Kovach & Rosenstiel, 2021), an increasing share of accessible information is produced by nonjournalistic sources and disseminated via social media, alternative and partisan media, and websites from governmental agencies, commercial businesses, think tanks, nongovernmental organizations, and so on. It has also become much easier for political and economic actors, including domestic or foreign malign actors, that push certain agendas and that are not committed to any norms of accuracy to reach out directly to the audience without having to go through traditional news media. An increasing share of information consequently never passes the news media's gates and has not been verified before being made public. Instead of functioning as gatekeepers, traditional news media have increasingly become gatewatchers (Bruns, 2018).

From a democratic perspective, digitalization and the evolution of high-choice media environments can thus be described as Janus-faced. On the one hand, there is a greater prevalence and accessibility of high-quality news and other types of information. It has never been as easy for people to inform themselves about nearly *any* topic. On the other hand, there is a greater prevalence and likelihood of people being exposed to false and misleading information. This includes intentionally deceptive information (disinformation), such as propaganda and fake news, as well as rumors or other information that is false or misleading but without any intent to mislead (misinformation; Benkler et al., 2018; Lecheler & Egelhofer, 2022). It also includes information, including conspiracy theories, where the intention to mislead may be hard to discern, but the information is nevertheless false and misleading (Butter, 2020; Önnerfors & Krouwel, 2021; Uscinski & Parent, 2014).

All this matters from a democratic perspective, as it is essential that people are sufficiently informed about politics and society (Dahl, 1998; Hochschild & Einstein, 2015; Milner, 2002). Although there are disagreements on exactly how and what type of knowledge people need (Lupia, 2016; Patterson, 2013; Zaller, 2003), there is broad scholarly consensus that at least some knowledge of politics and society is necessary for people to make informed political decisions, cast votes that reflect their true preferences and interests, hold those in power accountable, and participate meaningfully in political life (Dahl, 1998; Delli Carpini & Keeter, 1996; Milner, 2002). Thus, it is essential that people are neither *uninformed* nor *misinformed* (Kuklinski et al., 2000).

Since different types of news media are the main source of information about politics and society (Mitchell et al., 2016; Newman et al., 2023), the role of news media in informing people is of crucial democratic importance (Aalberg & Curran, 2012). Numerous studies from different countries have also demonstrated that people who consume more news media typically have more knowledge about politics and society than others and learn from using news media (Aalberg & Curran, 2012; Castro et al., 2022; Drew & Weaver, 2006; Eveland, 2001; Shehata et al., 2015), although not all news media and media platforms are equally informative (e.g., Fraile & Iyengar, 2014; Soroka et al., 2013; Strömbäck, 2017). Hence, it might seem safe to conclude that news media, despite different shortcomings, overall contribute positively to democracy by informing people. By news media, we refer to traditional or legacy news media such as newspapers and television news, regardless of whether they are published offline or online.

Such a conclusion may, however, be premature for five reasons. First, much of the extant research was completed when media choice was more restricted than in contemporary high-choice media environments. Since then, the share of the overall media supply that constitutes news has decreased, while the share of media supply that constitutes apolitical information and entertainment has increased (Hindman, 2009; Prior, 2007; Van Aelst et al., 2017). This has allowed for greater selective exposure based on people's political interest and has, accordingly, been accompanied by a rise in news avoidance (Skovsgaard & Andersen, 2020; Toff et al., 2024). Increasing economic pressure and competition for audiences may also have weakened the quality of journalism in traditional news media (Hamilton, 2004; Nielsen & Ganter, 2022; Usher, 2021). As a consequence, citizens, and mainly those with lower levels of education, have become more vulnerable in terms of gathering enough political information (Bergström et al., 2019; Blekesaune et al., 2012; Haugsgjerd et al., 2021).

Second, an increasing share of information originating from traditional news media is disseminated through social media, where the learning effects generally are weaker (Amsalem & Zoizner, 2023; de Zúñiga et al., 2024; Shehata & Strömbäck, 2021). Relatedly, a large share of information on social media, especially from political alternative or partisan media, is biased and intended to persuade or confirm people's pre-existing beliefs and identities rather than to inform (Benkler et al., 2018; Cushion, 2024; Garrett et al., 2016; Weeks, 2024). In countries where mainstream media have been more or less captured by illiberal political actors, those media are also involved in disseminating false and misleading information (Štětka & Mihelj, 2024).

Third, while traditional news media, in general, seek to provide information that is verified and truthful (Kovach & Rosenstiel, 2021), they are typically heavily reliant on statements and information provided by political elites (Bennett et al., 2007; Cook, 2005). At the same time, as evidenced by Donald Trump, there are signs that political elites increasingly are the sources of false and misleading information or use false and misleading information as political weapons (Albrecht, 2023; Bergmann, 2025; Kessler et al., 2020). This creates a challenge for traditional news media, whose job partly is to report on elite statements. This, too, may lead traditional news media to become part of the dissemination of false and misleading information (Thorson, 2024a; Tsfati et al., 2020).

Fourth, most research on learning effects from using media has focused on facts that are rather uncontroversial and uncontested. At the same time, research suggests that we live in a state of post-truth, where the political debate is increasingly focused on framing what is true and what is not, and is characterized by polarization over what constitutes facts and truths (Glüer & Wikforss, 2022; McIntyre, 2018; Rekker, 2021; Strömbäck, Boomgaarden et al., 2022; Young, 2023). This triggers motivated reasoning and confirmation biases (Kunda, 1990; Lodge & Taber, 2013; Nickerson, 1998; Thorson, 2024b; Young, 2023). This implies that learning effects may differ depending on whether the facts are uncontested or not, and that media use may, in fact, lead to misperceptions instead of correct knowledge (Damstra et al., 2023; Flynn et al., 2017; Lindgren et al., 2022).

Fifth, although there are important exceptions (e.g., Aalberg & Curran, 2012; Castro et al., 2022; Soroka et al., 2013), there is a general lack of cross-national comparative research, particularly including potential learning effects from using different types of both traditional media, such as upmarket and mass-market newspapers and television, and newer media, such as social media and messaging apps. This implies that the generalizability and conditionality of findings from previous research remain unclear.

Taken together, this raises several key questions that are at the heart of this Element. In contemporary high-choice media environments, (1) how are people's knowledge and perceptions of politics and society influenced by their use of different types of media, (2) are there any differences depending on whether facts are contested or not, and (3) what differences exist between lower- and higher-educated citizens and across countries?

1.1 The Twin Challenge of Increasing Media Choice

While many optimists in the early days of digitalization posited that the Internet and digital media would strengthen democracy by, among other things, breaking down the barriers to the public sphere, letting more voices be heard, increasing the flow and availability of information, and facilitating political participation (Jenkins, 2006; Negroponte, 1995; Norris, 2000), over time, such optimism has been replaced by a more pessimistic – or perhaps realistic – outlook (Bail, 2021; Persily & Tucker, 2020; Prior, 2007; Young, 2023). With respect to people's knowledge and perceptions of politics and society, there are two main concerns that are recurring in contemporary theory and research.

First, there is the "old" concern that some people remain *uninformed* about politics and society, despite the abundance of news and other information. The rise of digital media and the multiplication and subsequent fragmentation of media channels require people's motivation to find and select suitable information. Additionally, for people who are less interested in news about politics and society, it has become easier to opt out of using news media (Andersen et al., 2024; Prior, 2007; Skovsgaard & Andersen, 2020). Research also suggests an increasing share of news avoiders over time, that is, people who seldom or never follow the news through using news media (Espeland, 2024; Ksiazek et al., 2010; Strömbäck et al., 2013; Toff & Kalogeropoulos, 2020), although there are differences across countries (Castro et al., 2022; Toff & Kalogeropoulos, 2020; Villi et al., 2022). News avoidance may be particularly common among younger people (Elvestad & Phillips, 2018) and people with lower levels of education (Bergström et al., 2019; Haugsgjerd et al., 2021). Instead, different social media platforms have become more important as sources of information. At the same time, research recurrently shows that people learn significantly less from social media than from traditional media (Amsalem & Zoizner, 2023; Shehata & Strömbäck, 2021; Van Aelst et al., 2025; van Erkel & Van Aelst, 2021), even though they may think or feel that they learn (Leonhard et al., 2020; Schäfer & Schemer, 2024). It is also not clear whether the classical insight that television news and newspapers help inform people about politics holds true in media environments where economic pressures are tougher than ever, and many news media are forced to produce more with continuous deadlines but with ever fewer journalists and decreasing resources for newsgathering and verifying information (Hamilton, 2004; Nielsen & Ganter, 2022; Usher, 2021).

Second, and more recently, there are growing concerns that people might base their beliefs on false and misleading information disseminated through various media and thereby become *misinformed* (Grinberg et al., 2019; Hameleers, 2021; Humprecht et al., 2020; Rojecki & Meraz, 2016; Thorson, 2024a). In particular, since the 2016 US presidential election and the UK Brexit referendum, the role of digital, partisan, and political alternative media, as well as social media, in spreading misinformation has been at the center of scholarly research (Benkler et al., 2018; Broda & Strömbäck, 2024; Flynn et al., 2017; Weeks, 2024). All such dissemination of false and misleading information is problematic, since there may be a demand for false and misleading information if such information is aligned with people's already-held beliefs, perceptions, and identities (Štětka & Mihelj, 2024; Weeks, 2024; Young, 2023). This, in turn, can be explained by directional motivated reasoning and confirmation bias, which lead people to (unconsciously) prefer attitude-consistent information, even if such information may be false and misleading. Directional motivated reasoning and confirmation bias also lead people to biased information processing, even though people might think they are being rational (Kunda, 1990; Lodge & Taber, 2013; Nickerson, 1998). False and misleading information may thereby strengthen or lead to misperceptions and knowledge resistance (Glüer & Wikforss, 2022; Hameleers, 2021; Strömbäck, Wikforss et al., 2022; Young, 2023). This, in turn, may have far-reaching consequences at both the societal and individual level, as can be exemplified by the spread of and beliefs in misinformation during the COVID-19 pandemic (Bruns et al., 2020; Fotakis & Simou, 2023; Naeem et al., 2021) or the widespread false claims of and beliefs in voter fraud in the US in recent years (Berlinski et al., 2023; Eggers et al., 2021; Enders et al., 2021).

The twin challenge of increasing media choice thus seems to be that people may remain *un*informed about politics and society (because of lower use of traditional media, but also due to information overload) or become *mis*informed (because of the increasing prevalence of false and misleading information on – in particular – digital and social media platforms). However, while it is unclear whether or to what extent such worries are warranted, our understanding of such phenomena may also vary across political and social contexts, as we discuss below.

1.2 The Twin Challenge from a Comparative Perspective

In the past three decades, there has been a growing body of research emphasizing that understanding political communication phenomena from a comparative perspective is crucial. This research highlights how country-level factors might shape the relationship between citizens and their information environment (Castro et al., 2022; Esser & Hanitzsch, 2012). Such macro-level factors can shape both the supply and the demand side. Focusing on the supply side, the political information citizens encounter on a daily basis from traditional and social media can vary in quality and quantity depending on the local context. For example, some media systems have, in the past, been characterized by more favorable opportunity structures for knowledge acquisition than others, offering high-quality political information (Aalberg & Curran, 2012; Esser et al., 2012; Soroka et al., 2013).

In addition, the use of digital and social media for news is more widespread in some countries than in others, but the prevalence of correct as well as false and misleading information may vary, which, in turn, should influence the effects on learning and misperceptions (Castro et al., 2022). Furthermore, in many Western democracies, public service media have been shown to have an ecological effect on other news media channels, in the sense that they influence the quality and programming of news reporting also in commercial channels (Aalberg & Cushion, 2016; Castro-Herrero et al., 2018). Thereby, they offer people greater opportunities for exposure to high-quality news and diverse political viewpoints, both directly and indirectly (Bos et al., 2016; Shehata et al., 2015).

Macro-level factors can also shape the demand side, that is, citizens' motivations and abilities to engage with and learn from the information environment they live in. For example, the level of political control over public and commercial media may not only shape what type of information will normally appear in these outlets but also influence how different media are perceived by citizens as sources of credible information (Soroka et al., 2013; Štětka & Mihelj, 2024; Szostek, 2018b). Moreover, country-level education performance can also affect local citizens' abilities to learn from political content as well as their susceptibility to misperceptions when exposed to false information (Karlsen et al., 2020; Liu & Eveland, 2005).

Due to the importance of this comparative perspective, we not only examine the relationship between modern information environments and knowledge across all eighteen countries in our sample, but also devote special attention to testing how these relationships vary according to different national contexts.

1.3 Outline of the Element

To address these concerns, the overall purpose of this Element is to investigate the linkage between the use of different types of media on the one hand and both (a) knowledge and (b) misperceptions on the other across eighteen democracies. The countries selected are all situated in the Global North. While this admittedly entails a Western bias, as in so much other media and communication research, it will allow us to investigate this relationship across a wider set of countries than in most other studies. As the relationship between media use, knowledge, and misperceptions might differ both across and within countries, we will furthermore also investigate the moderating role of individual- and country-level education and press freedom.

In the next section, we will describe the methodology and data that we use. We devote extra attention to the way we selected survey questions on general political knowledge and on contested issue knowledge or misperceptions, so that they are comparable across countries. Section 3 delves deeper into the relationship between different types of media and political knowledge, while Section 4 does the same for misperceptions. Section 5 further explores the relationship between political knowledge and the difference between upmarket and mass-market media. In all these sections, we devote ample attention to describing the consistency of the findings across countries. In Section 6, we take an even more systematic approach by focusing on two macro-level factors: press freedom and countries' education performance, as important characteristics to explain variation across countries. In Section 7, we offer our conclusions, discuss the limitations of our study, and suggest avenues for future research.

2 Methodology and Data

2.1 Sample and Data Collection

For the empirical analyses in this Element, we rely on a dataset retrieved from an online survey focusing on individuals' political information environment. The data was collected within the research project "The Threats and Potentials of a Changing Political Information Environment" (Threatpie). Fielding took place in eighteen countries between May 3 and June 24, 2022, and was conducted by Kantar Lightspeed. We recruited 1,500 participants from each of the following countries: Austria, Czech Republic, Denmark, France, Germany, Greece, Israel, Italy, Netherlands, Norway, Poland, Romania, Spain, Sweden, the UK, and the US. Additionally, 1,000 participants were recruited in the dominant linguistic regions of Switzerland (German) and Belgium (Flemish). The total sample size was $N = 26{,}000$.

While these countries share similarities in terms of being Western democracies and part of the Global North, they also differ in terms of media systems, levels of press freedom, strength of democratic institutions, and social and cultural backgrounds (Hallin & Mancini, 2004; Humprecht et al., 2022). Moreover, this sample allows us to explore diverse media consumption habits in the audience, as there is an abundance of traditional and digital media sources in each country that individuals can choose from to obtain political information.

The cooperation rate in each country was generally high, ranging between 79 percent in the US and 95 percent in Italy. A quality check was implemented to filter out participants who did not read the questions attentively. Quotas were implemented for gender, age, and education during the participant recruitment process to obtain a sample that resembles each respective country's population. However, a comparison with census data revealed that individuals with lower educational degrees were underrepresented in some countries, that is, Greece, Norway, Israel, and Sweden. On the other hand, there was an overrepresentation of participants with low education in the UK, Switzerland, Poland, the Czech Republic, and Belgium. The use of weights to compensate for the underrepresentation or overrepresentation of specific groups does not alter the substantive findings.

The original questionnaire was in English. Where available, we used translations of existing scales to create questionnaires for the online survey in all languages. The translations were reviewed by experts in each country involved in the project.

2.2 Measures

2.2.1 Measuring Political Knowledge and Misperceptions

The primary goal of our study is to examine how media use shapes knowledge on contested and noncontested issues. We therefore measured people's knowledge of political facts as well as the more contested issues of COVID-19 and climate change across eighteen countries. One challenge, though, is how to measure knowledge. Most studies that measure people's political knowledge using surveys typically ask respondents to correctly answer questions in the domains of interest. The most common approach in the literature is to construct a simple additive index that counts the number of correct answers, which is then taken to indicate respondents' knowledge levels (e.g., one correct answer out of four indicates less knowledge, and four correct answers indicate high knowledge). However, using this approach to tap into respondents' knowledge is not unproblematic from a methodological perspective, particularly with respect to cross-national studies.

First, some knowledge items may be relatively easy to answer, resulting in a limited measure of knowledge that cannot differentiate well between respondents with high versus low knowledge levels. Second, summative knowledge scores may ignore the fact that items might vary in difficulty and should therefore have different weights in a knowledge construct. Third, summing up correct responses overlooks the issue of measurement error. At the same time, measurement error can severely bias the estimates of regression models depending on the nature of the bias. More specifically, measurement error that varies randomly likely results in underestimation of true relationships or effects, while nonrandom measurement error can bias results, and it is difficult to predict in what direction findings are biased. Fourth, and most challenging, measuring knowledge in a comparative study requires tapping the same latent ability (i.e., knowledge) across very different contexts. Due to cultural, social, and political characteristics, what is considered vital political knowledge in one country might, however, be less relevant in other countries. For instance, media coverage of a given issue can vary widely in different countries, thereby directly shaping people's access to political information regarding this issue. In other words, the measurement of knowledge across contexts may vary due to external factors regardless of individual abilities. This requires scholars to carefully think of knowledge measures that are comparable across countries.

One way to address these methodological issues, as suggested by the pioneers in measuring political knowledge, Delli Carpini and Keeter (1993), is to use *Item Response Theory* (IRT). One key benefit of IRT is that it takes into account the fact that knowledge items not only correlate but also differ in difficulty. Therefore, we use IRT (i.e., 2PL models and graded response models) for scaling, which treats respondents' level of knowledge as a function of both their own ability and question difficulty (van der Linden & Hambleton, 1997). More concretely, IRT helps improve tests or surveys designed to measure knowledge or abilities by evaluating each question (or "item") individually. It assesses how difficult each question is – easy questions are answered correctly by most people, while harder ones are only solved by a few. IRT also considers how well each question differentiates between people with different levels of knowledge, ensuring that questions help distinguish between someone who knows a lot and someone who knows less. Models like the 1PL (one-parameter logistic) model focus only on difficulty, while the 2PL (two-parameter logistic) model adds discrimination, which measures how well a question separates individuals with varying levels of knowledge. IRT models can also be used to deal with multinomial or ordered-categorical variables. By focusing on questions that provide the most information about a person's knowledge, IRT allows for more precise and efficient measurements with fewer questions. The results of our IRT analyses[1] and how they were taken into account will be described below.

2.2.2 Political Knowledge

Important in the context of this study is that there are different definitions of *political knowledge*, which might influence the results of any study. One common approach is to focus on current affairs or surveillance-knowledge, which refers to people's knowledge about recent news or events (Allcott et al., 2019; Shehata & Strömbäck, 2021; van Erkel & Van Aelst, 2021) or on issue-specific knowledge, which taps into people's understanding of specific policy domains in their local political context (Anspach et al., 2019). While providing important information on what people know about day-to-day events, operationalizing political knowledge according to these definitions raises several challenges in comparative studies. As noted above, people's knowledge of political events can be significantly influenced by factors that vary across countries and beyond individual capabilities. Contextual confounders, like media coverage and issue salience, make it difficult to compare knowledge on various national-level events across countries (see also Haugsgjerd et al., 2021). To address this challenge, we define and operationalize political knowledge as *general knowledge*, which refers to the extent to which people know about important political institutions and the main actors in those institutions (Damstra et al., 2023; Gil de Zúñiga et al., 2012). However, to keep a link with media coverage, we selected general questions that were related to recent events, such as the COVID-19 pandemic (e.g., a question related to the minister of health) and the war in Ukraine (e.g., a question related to NATO), which received at least some news coverage in the period under study. Table 1 details the four identical knowledge items provided to respondents in all eighteen countries (translated into the local language). The degree of political knowledge was assessed by four single-choice questions with four answer options each. Correct answers were recoded to "1," and incorrect answers, including the "don't know" option, were recoded to "0." As in most studies on political knowledge, we considered people who do not know the answer as being *uninformed*. However, we are aware that some people more easily guess the correct answer than others (e.g., men more than women), and that this may influence some results (e.g., gender differences) (Mondak & Anderson, 2004).

---

[1] For the IRT analysis, we relied on Stata 17.0 SE (StataCorp, 2021) and *mirt* package in R (Chalmers, 2012).

Table 1 Political knowledge items used in the surveys and the final analyses.

Item number	Statement in survey	% of correct answers
1	"Who is the Secretary of State for Health and Social Care?"	58.5
2	"Who is the current General Secretary of the United Nations (UN)?"	35.0
3	"Which of the following countries does not belong to the North Atlantic Treaty Organization (NATO)?"	60.5
4	"Who leads the European Commission at the moment?"	50.6

As our general knowledge items used in this comparative study were broadly related to events and persons that appeared in the news in the months before the survey, they depend less on short-term factors such as exposure to traditional and social media and are traditionally associated with long-term factors related to education levels or general political sophistication (Haugsgjerd et al., 2021; van Erkel & Van Aelst, 2021). Because of this, our measure of general political knowledge can be said to provide a conservative test of the relationship between media use and knowledge. In other words, any relationship we observe between these two variables is likely weaker than the impact of media use on more day-to-day political knowledge (Fraile & Iyengar, 2014).

Figure 1 presents item characteristic curves per country, utilizing 2PL models and thereby taking both difficulty and discrimination into account. The y-axis represents the probability of answering each item correctly, while the x-axis represents the latent trait (knowledge on noncontested political issues). The standardized center value (0) represents an average knowledge level of the sample, with values on the right indicating higher-than-average knowledge, and values on the left indicating lower-than-average knowledge.

The examination of the item characteristic curves (ICCs) in Figure 1 suggests that most items behave similarly across all countries. Most of them are characterized by a positively steep S-shaped curve, suggesting good *discrimination*, that is, the ability to distinguish between respondents with low and high levels of knowledge. Differences in the steepness of the ICCs indicate variations in the ability of items across countries to discriminate between different levels of knowledge.

Figure 1 also informs us about the *difficulty* of the knowledge items in each country. To assess how difficult an item is, one can look at the point on the x-axis where the curve of a specific item intersects the 50 percent probability level on

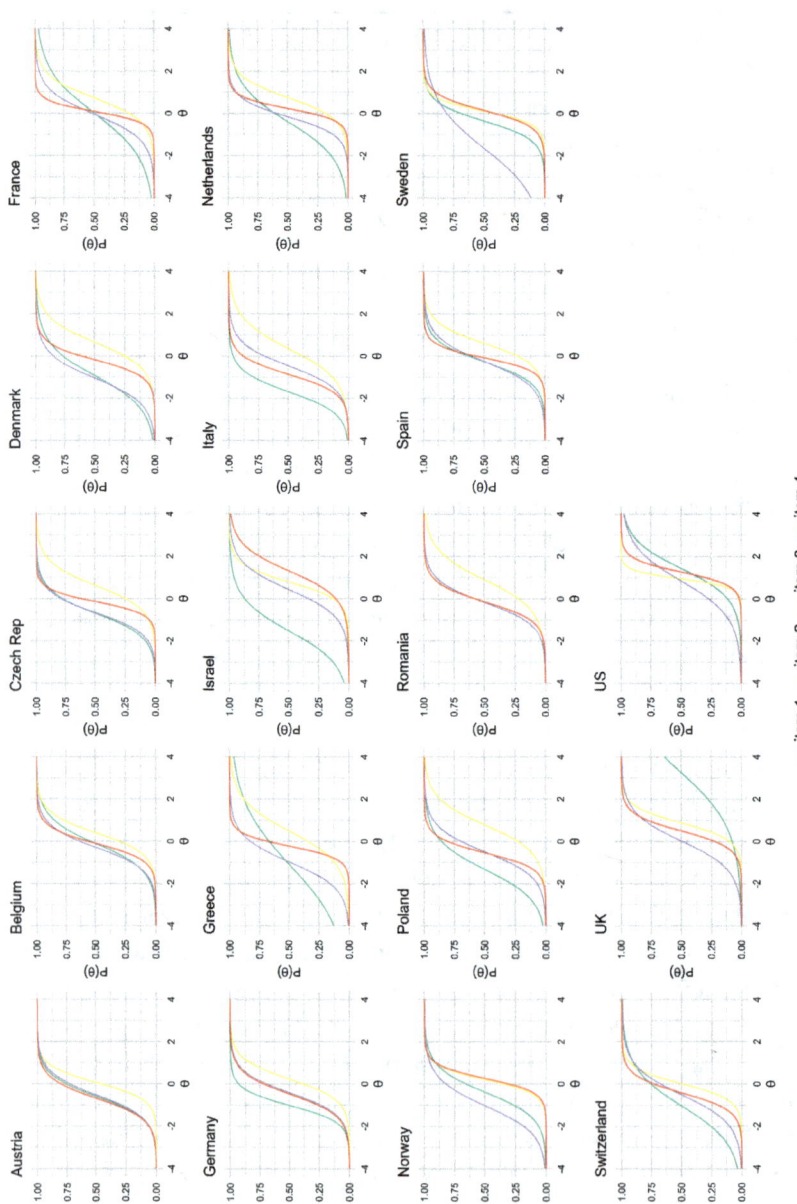

Figure 1 Item characteristic curves for 2PL models per country, using four items tapping general political knowledge.[2]

[2] Due to a survey fielding error in Romania, none of the answers provided on item 1 were correct (see item wording in Table 1). In other words, Romanian respondents could not answer this question correctly. Therefore, this item was removed from the figure and the analyses in the Element, and the Romanian knowledge scale only relies on three items.

the *y*-axis. If the intersection point with the 50 percent probability on the *y*-axis is located to the left of 0, that is, in the area of negative values on the *x*-axis (i.e., lower levels of knowledge), this indicates that the item is easy to answer correctly – since even those with less knowledge abilities are more likely to provide correct answers. One can observe that knowledge items 1 and 2 were relatively easy to answer in many countries, as the intersection point is to the left of the 0 value (average knowledge) on the *x*-axis (e.g., Denmark, Israel, Norway). However, none of the items are either extremely easy or extremely difficult to answer in any country. Therefore, we decided to keep all knowledge items in the final scale construction and in our analysis.

2.2.3 Misperceptions of Contested Issues

While most research on the relationship between media use and knowledge traditionally focused on uncontested issues or facts, in recent years, research has increasingly shifted toward people's knowledge of issues that are highly prone to political contestation, such as global warming, vaccines, and genetically modified foods and crops (e.g., Arechar et al., 2023; Lindgren et al., 2022; Vliegenthart et al., 2023). Most research in this area has however focused on single countries and/or single issues, meaning that our understanding of how to compare knowledge about contested issues across countries with different political and social cleavages remains limited.

Our project, in contrast, investigates the comparability of contested knowledge across countries within two highly debated issue domains: COVID-19 and climate change. We chose these topics because they were, at the time of data collection, high-priority issues in media and public discussions in all countries under observation. Additionally, these issues are highly politicized in the sense that, despite broad scientific consensus, different ideological camps in different countries doubt the truth status of certain claims or even promote false claims, thereby increasing the controversy in the public (Damstra et al., 2023).

Following previous research (Damstra et al., 2023; Strömbäck et al., 2023), we asked respondents to rate eight statements related to these topics, relying on a scale ranging from 1 ("very certain it is false") to 5 ("very certain it is true"; with 3 being the "don't know" option). For the wording of the statements, see Table 2. In line with previous research on misperceptions (Damstra et al., 2023; Nyhan & Reifler, 2010; Pennycook et al., 2018), we recoded respondents' answers so that higher values represent higher levels of misperceptions. Depending on the veracity of each item and the original answers ("very certain it is false," "somewhat certain it is false," "don't know," "very certain it is true," "somewhat certain it is true"), we then created misperception indicators on 5-point-scales: "certainly informed" (1),

Table 2 Misperception items used in the surveys and final analyses rated on a scale from 1 (very certain it is false) to 5 (very certain it is true).

Topic	Item number	Statement in survey	Used in the final analyses	% probably/ certainly correct (% don't know)
Climate change	1	"The global temperature is rising"		88 (4)
	2	"Human activity is an important contributing factor to global warming"		83 (5)
	3	"Climate change occurs because of changes in the Earth's solar orbit, and not because of fossil fuels"	V	51 (13)
	4	"Climate change is the main cause of natural disasters"		76 (6)
COVID-19	5	"Strokes are a common side effect of COVID-19 vaccines"	V	51 (19)
	6	"COVID-19 vaccines are safe for pregnant women"	V	50 (20)
	7	"COVID-19 vaccines can change your DNA"	V	62 (16)
	8	"COVID-19 vaccines protect you 100% against the virus"		66 (5)

Note. While we presented all eight statements to respondents, the final variable construction was based only on items 3, 5, 6, and 7, based on IRT analyses.

"somewhat informed" (2), "don't know" (3), "somewhat misinformed" (4), and "certainly misinformed" (5). We acknowledge that our measurement of being *misinformed* (using a scale) follows a different logic than being *uninformed* (using a dummy variable). In particular, the people who answered "don't know" on these statements were considered as being in doubt on these contested issues and therefore placed in the middle on an informed–misinformed continuum.

The more complex nature of measuring misperceptions is also evident in our selection of items. Out of the original eight survey items, in the end we retained only four indicators based on several criteria. First, we excluded item 4 ("Climate change is the main cause of natural disasters") because changes in the assessments of the Intergovernmental Panel on Climate Change (IPCC) have made the veracity of the statement scientifically debatable. This has made the statement unsuitable for assessing respondent accuracy. Second, we used an IRT graded response model to analyze response patterns and the quality of each item in measuring contested knowledge across and within countries. Figure 2 shows category characteristic curves for each of the seven items across countries. Basically, the figure represents the probability of participants responding with each of the categories, that is, certainly correct (red curve), probably correct (orange curve), don't know (purple curve), probably incorrect (green curve), and certainly incorrect (blue curve). Specifically, certainly correct responses are reflective of small values of the latent trait misperceptions, while certainly incorrect responses occur for high values of the latent trait. Steep category characteristic curves are desirable because they indicate higher discrimination in terms of misperceptions.

As can be seen, items 3, 5, 6, and 7 show the best fit to our assumption that misperceptions are a latent trait that ranges from correct responses to incorrect ones, with "do not know" responses falling in between. The category characteristic curves for these items correspond to this pattern. In contrast, item 8 showed a response pattern that differed from the others, indicating a lack of one-dimensionality if it was included. Additionally, for items 1 and 2, we observe that misperceptions were reported infrequently (less than 10 percent of the responses), and more than 80 percent of the respondents reported correct responses. Therefore, the category characteristic curve for incorrect responses is not very good at discriminating individuals with moderate or high levels of misperceptions. This becomes obvious when the steepness of the blue category characteristic curves for these items is compared with the corresponding category characteristic curves of items 3, 5, 6, and 7. Because of the skewed distribution, these items were deemed not suitable for the modeling of misperceptions. Overall, we are therefore left with four items that demonstrate acceptable response patterns for a measure of misperceptions across the sample of

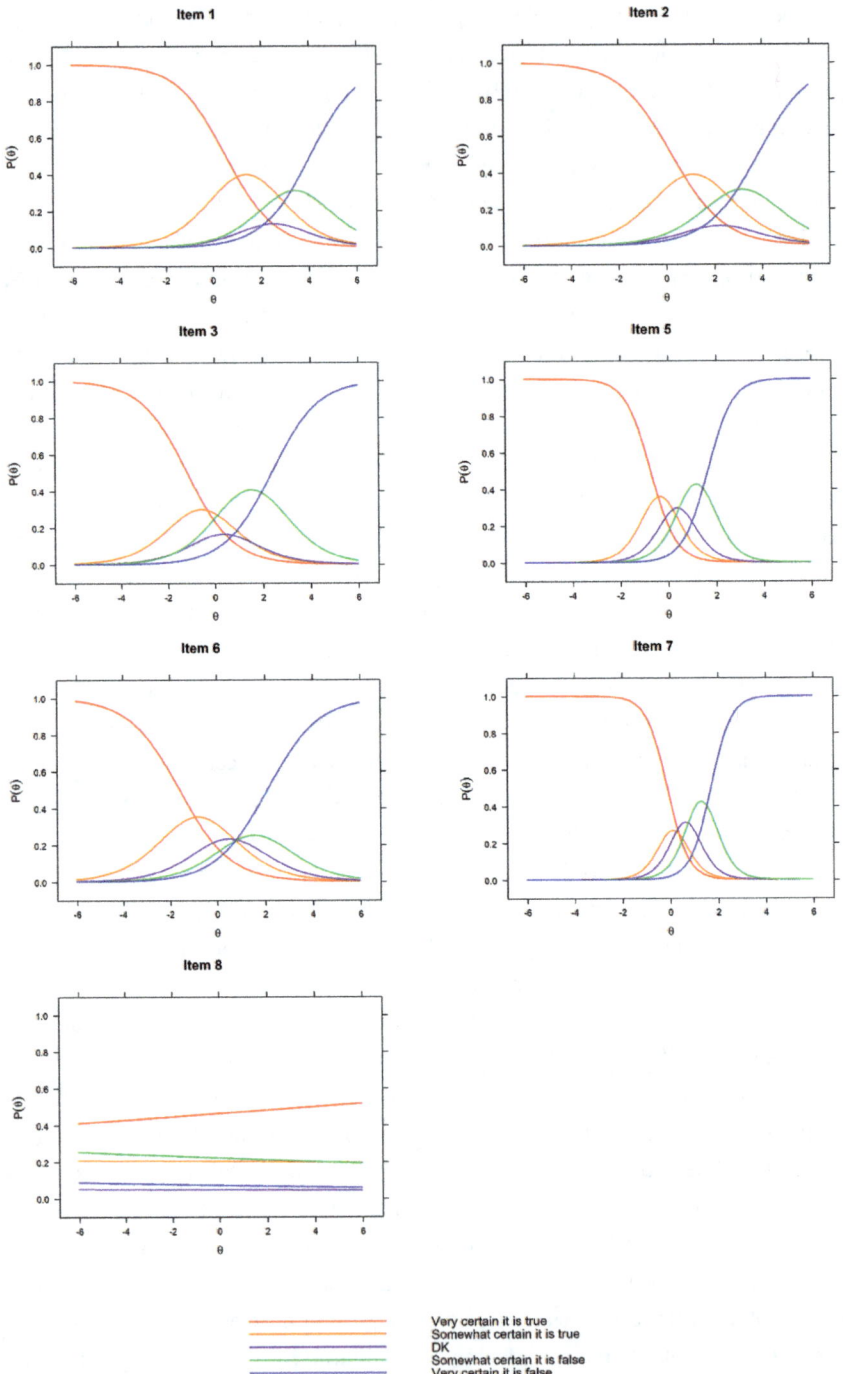

Figure 2 Category characteristic curves for the graded response model across countries.

eighteen countries. Therefore, we only include items 3, 5, 6, and 7 in our final measure of misperceptions.

2.2.4 Media Use

The key independent variable in our analyses is media use. To investigate this, the survey asked about which general media genres respondents use but also about the specific media outlets respondents consume. More precisely, respondents were asked where in their everyday life and how often they got information about political news and current affairs (e.g., migration, environment, or health). The response alternatives included different *media types*, such as TV, radio, newspapers and magazines, news aggregators (e.g., Google News, Yahoo News, etc.), social media sites (e.g., Facebook, Twitter, etc.), and messaging services (e.g., WhatsApp, Telegram, Facebook Messenger). In each case, participants were asked to rate their news use on a scale ranging from 1 (Never) to 6 (Daily). These news genre questions were the same for all countries.

News Types

Based on the types of media used for informational purposes, TV and newspapers were selected as representatives of traditional news media, while social media sites and messaging services were selected as newer media types to be compared in their impact on political knowledge and misperceptions.

Media Channels

Besides news types, participants were asked to indicate how frequently they used specific news media outlets from a list that contained fifteen to twenty popular outlets, depending on the participant's country. The response scale ranged from 1 (Never) to 6 (Daily). The full list, including the recoded variables, can be found in the Online Appendix.

Public Service versus Commercial Broadcasting

From the list of information sources, TV outlets were categorized as either public service or commercial (where applicable). The measure thus describes the frequency of each participant's use of public service versus commercial TV news shows in their respective country.

Upmarket versus Mass-Market Newspapers

For newspapers, the same procedure as for broadcast was applied. From the country-specific list of news outlets described earlier, the newspapers were classified as either upmarket (targeting a more "elite" audience of higher-educated news users with longer articles and more hard news) or popular or mass-market papers (targeting a broader segment of the population with shorter news stories and more soft news). Since the distinction is not as clear-cut as it is for broadcast media, experts from each country supported us in the categorization process. Consequently, the frequency of participants' use of upmarket/mass-market newspapers in their respective country was measured.

2.3 Education and the Conditional Nature of Learning via News Media

As argued by Delli Carpini and Keeter (1996), political knowledge, just like economic wealth, is not equally distributed among the public, and if we want to establish the effect of media, it is crucial to understand the role of certain characteristics that might explain variation in political knowledge. In this regard, education has proven to be a key factor in explaining political knowledge (Delli Carpini & Keeter, 1996; Grönlund & Milner, 2006). In general, higher-educated people have greater cognitive ability and more training and practice in processing information (Liu & Eveland, 2005). Therefore, scholars have frequently identified a "knowledge gap" between lower and higher-educated citizens, a gap that is generally widened by media use (Lind & Boomgaarden, 2019; Tichenor et al., 1970), mainly because people with low levels of education may also have less access to sources of political information and fewer skills to follow complex political issues in the news (Karlsen et al., 2020). Furthermore, the less educated often avoid news or consume lower-quality news (Haugsgjerd et al., 2021). In other words, by using media, the informationally rich get richer, while the lower-educated remain information poor (Price & Zaller, 1993) – often referred to as a Matthew effect (Kümpel, 2020).

However, some aspects of the role of media in deepening the existing knowledge gap remain unclear or unanswered. First, research has shown that different traditional media channels might have different effects. Most (but not all) studies found that newspaper use widens knowledge gaps, while TV news use appears to temper (or maintain) existing educational inequalities (e.g., Eveland & Scheufele, 2000; Jerit et al., 2006). This is mainly due to the higher cognitive effort that newspaper reading requires compared to watching television news (Graber, 1990). In that respect, it is highly unclear how the role of social media, combining video, images, and short pieces of text, should be understood. Lind & Boomgaarden (2019) showed in their meta-analysis that online media strengthen existing educational inequalities, but research on social media and messaging apps is, so far, missing. The authors also note that the few studies that focused on knowledge about contested issues and misbeliefs did not confirm the existence of a knowledge gap. Although this study is not a test of the knowledge gap hypothesis, we want to contribute to this debate by analyzing the moderating role of educational inequalities in studying the relationship between (old and newer) media use and political knowledge.

2.4 Covariates and Controls

Aside from education, there are also other characteristics that might explain variation in political knowledge. First, people's motivation determines if and how much they learn. A key dimension of motivation in this area is political interest, since it affects the time and effort individuals devote to politics (Prior, 2019; Strömbäck et al., 2013). We will also control for age, which may affect political learning. Many adolescents and young adults are devoted to social media platforms and (alternative) news sites as their most important source of political information (Andersen et al., 2021). These sources not only provide less political content but are also often seen as a breeding ground for misinformation (Theocharis et al., 2023). Finally, we control for political ideology on a left-right continuum, since ideology is an important factor that can shape people's willingness to be exposed to political information and to believe in false information (Garrett & Bond, 2021; Jost et al., 2009).

To ease the comparison across coefficients in the models that predict political knowledge and misperceptions, we normalized all independent variables. We used a min-max normalization, which results in all independent variables having the same scale length, ranging from 0 to 1.

2.5 Analytical Strategy

To model political knowledge, we rely on structural equation modeling (SEM), in which political knowledge is estimated as a latent variable using the dichotomous items as reflective indicators. In other words, differences in political knowledge as the latent ability are assumed to cause different responses to the selected knowledge questions. This model is equivalent to the IRT 2PL model that was used for the item analysis. The only difference is that the IRT restricts the variance of the latent trait to 1. This restriction is relaxed in the SEM since we want to predict variation in the latent variable political knowledge using the predictors described earlier.

Most previous research has typically used the responses to the included knowledge questions and summarized correct responses to form a continuous political knowledge score. This procedure overlooks two important issues, however. First, a summary score assumes that all knowledge items have the same weight. A look at the ICCs and CCCs clearly shows that the items differ in their difficulty and discrimination parameters. Put differently, when some questions are easier than others, we cannot treat them as equally important for a knowledge score. Second, the responses to knowledge questions are unlikely to reflect true scores but may be affected by measurement error. This measurement error can be systematic or random and stem from sloppy responding, strategic responding, misunderstanding of the questions, or guessing. Treating observed values as true scores ignores this problem.

The best way to address these issues is to rely on SEM, which accounts for different weights of items and measurement error (Bollen, 1989). This modeling reduces the standard errors of estimates and thereby increases the precision of regression estimates. The models that estimate the relationships between media use and political knowledge were multilevel SEMs using a binary logistic link function to model the relationship between latent variables and binary indicators. The multilevel component accounts for the nesting of individual respondents (Level 1) within countries (Level 2). The intra-class correlation is 0.12 for political knowledge, which indicates that 12 percent of the variance in political knowledge is due to differences between countries.

In a similar vein, we relied on a multilevel SEM in which contested knowledge is a latent construct based on reflective indicators 3, 5, 6, and 7. The scale of the items was assumed to be ordered-categorical. Therefore, we relied on an ordinal logistic link function to link the latent variable to the reflective indicators. We also accounted for the multilevel nature of the data for the prediction of misperceptions. The intra-class correlation coefficient was considerably lower for misperceptions: 0.03. In other words, only 3 percent of the variance in misperceptions was due to country differences. The covariates in all models were treated as observed variables, as most of them were measured with single items. The SEM was run in Stata 17 SE (StataCorp, 2021).

2.6 Overview of Political Knowledge and Misperceptions by Country

Although we are mainly interested in the relationship between media use within and across countries, it is informative to show the average scores on both measures across the countries under study. The political knowledge and misperception scores are estimates based on the IRT models and vary around the normed midpoint 0. Therefore, negative scores represent lower knowledge or misperceptions than the average of all countries and positive scores indicate higher-than-average knowledge or misperceptions. It should be noted, though, that we need to be careful when interpreting these differences, since the difficulty of questions varies between countries, as does the amount of attention given to some issues or

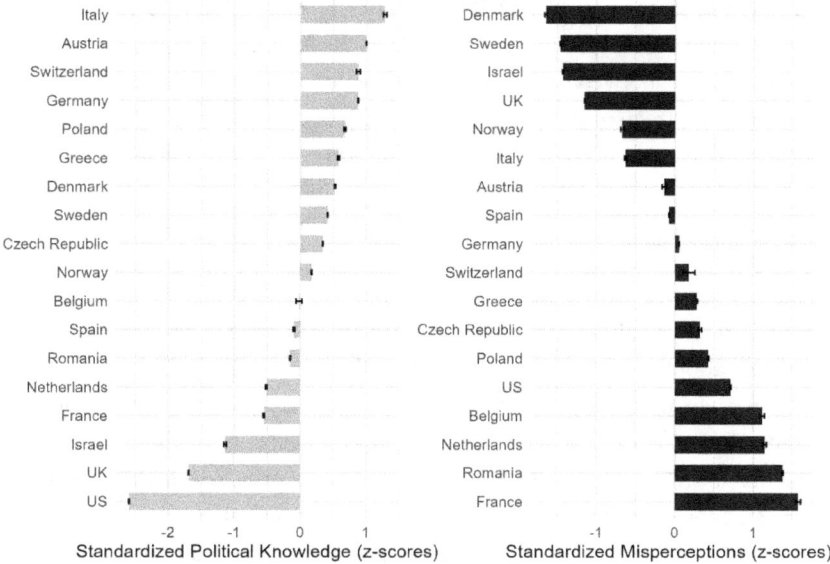

Figure 3 Mean political knowledge and misperception scores per country.

actors in the national news. For instance, the question about the leader of the European Commission was probably given less attention in the US or Israeli press than in most European countries. Therefore, participants in the US or in Israel are disadvantaged in this regard. Differences in samples are also likely to explain differences in political knowledge and misperceptions across countries. Still, the average knowledge score of the US respondents probably reflects the relatively low knowledge of international issues found in other studies (Aalberg & Curran, 2012; Iyengar et al., 2010). For example, less than 20 percent of participants from the US knew who the head of the US Department of Health was. In contrast, in other countries, between 50 percent and 90 percent of participants were able to correctly identify the secretary or minister of health in their respective countries. Figure 3 also shows that the variation across countries is higher for political knowledge than for misperceptions. However, even in the case of misperceptions, we must admit that both issues (COVID-19 and climate change) were controversial in all countries, but probably not equally "contested."

One thing that should be noted is that the correlational nature of the data does not allow us to establish the chain of causality. A positive relationship between media use and knowledge or (mis)perceptions might reflect a media effect, where levels of knowledge or (mis)perceptions are influenced by media use. It might, however, also reflect a selection effect, where levels of knowledge or (mis)perceptions influence media use. Based on extant theory and research

(Amsalem & Zoizner, 2023; Delli Carpini & Keeter, 1996; Fraile & Iyengar, 2014; Shehata & Strömbäck, 2021; Van Aelst et al., 2025), we believe, however, that associations between media use and knowledge or (mis)perceptions mainly reflect media effects rather than selection effects, in contrast to, for example, education that more clearly precedes media use.

3 News Use and Political Knowledge

3.1 Introduction

Turning to the analyses, a crucial way by which people can become more informed about politics is by following the news. Basically, by exposing themselves to political news coverage, people may learn about politics and current events, leading to gains in political knowledge. However, how people consume news has drastically changed. A growing group of people uses social media and messaging apps to inform themselves about what is happening. Still, traditional news media remain an important part of the media diet for many people. This raises the question of how much people learn from using both traditional and newer media. Below, we discuss previous research on this before presenting our data from eighteen countries.

3.2 Traditional and New Media and Political Knowledge

A recurrent finding in previous research is that people who consume more news and news media have more factual knowledge about the main political actors and current events and are typically better able to position political candidates and parties on different issues and ideological dimensions (Castro et al., 2022; Chaffee & Kanihan, 1997; Eveland, 2001; Schäfer & Schemer, 2024). These studies, often focusing on election campaigns, confirm that people learn from traditional news media, particularly from outlets and programs that pay special attention to the election campaign (Drew & Weaver, 2006; Shehata & Strömbäck, 2021; Skovsgaard et al., 2016; van der Meer et al., 2016). This is in line with the overall finding that the news media contribute to political knowledge acquisition, particularly when there is a high density of factual political information in the news coverage (De Vreese & Boomgaarden, 2006; Fraile & Iyengar, 2014; Jerit et al., 2006). More recent studies on the linkage between news repertoires and political knowledge also confirm that so-called 'news traditionalists' score higher in terms of current affairs knowledge than people with other news repertoires (Castro et al., 2022; Vliegenthart et al., 2023). In the context of our study, a general expectation is, hence, that following the news from traditional news media contributes to factual political knowledge.

The situation might be different with respect to social media. Although findings from previous research are not fully consistent, in general, extant research is quite pessimistic about the contribution of social media platforms to political learning. Although knowledge effects from using social media such as Facebook have been found in experimental settings (Bode, 2016) and when the absolute amount of news about political events on the platform has been measured (Edgerly et al., 2018), studies based on surveys typically find no or negative knowledge effects from using social media (de Zúñiga et al., 2024; Shehata & Strömbäck, 2021; Van Aelst et al., 2025). In fact, a recent meta-analysis of seventy-six studies found no evidence of meaningful political knowledge gains from social media use in observational studies, and relatively small learning effects in experiments (Amsalem & Zoizner, 2023). In some cases, platform-level differences have emerged, as scholars found a positive effect of using Twitter (e.g., Boukes, 2019; Park, 2017) but failed to find knowledge gains when Facebook as a source for following the news was considered.

There may be several reasons for these findings. Some suggest that the goal of finding political information on social media is typically subordinate to other primary goals, such as entertainment or social tie maintenance (Bode, 2016). While people may incidentally encounter political information on social media, substantive political learning will mostly occur when the topic at stake is relevant enough for the user (Nanz & Matthes, 2020). Others attribute the lack of political learning to the risk of information overload due to the abundant stream of algorithmically curated information on social media (van Erkel & Van Aelst, 2021). Still, others have found that the "news snacking" that is typical of social media may lead people to perceive that they are learning while, in fact, news snacking counteracts learning (Leonhard et al., 2020; Ohme & Mothes, 2020; Schäfer, 2020). Also important is that news about politics and current affairs typically constitutes a minuscule share of all content in most people's social media feeds. On a more general level, differences in attributes across media platforms in terms of the organization and structure of information and consumption patterns, in conjunction with the fact that social media are typically used on mobile phones, may all play a role (Andersen & Strömbäck, 2021; Ohme & Mothes, 2025; Schäfer & Schemer, 2024; Stroud et al., 2020).

In addition to social media, so-called messaging services, such as Facebook Messenger, WhatsApp, Snapchat, and Telegram, have also become gateways to political information. Although the relationship between these (mainly private) messaging services and politics has not yet been examined widely, the few studies that have been published suggest they are negatively associated with political knowledge (Gil De Zúñiga & Goyanes, 2023; Yamamoto et al., 2018).

Although more research is clearly needed, it seems that these channels mainly promote learning under specific circumstances. For instance, a study in Chile found that using WhatsApp to learn about public affairs had a modest, albeit significant, positive relationship with political knowledge (Valenzuela et al., 2023). An experimental study among adolescents in the Netherlands also found that WhatsApp can facilitate learning (Vermeer et al., 2021). However, in general, it seems that messaging services mostly contain more private and soft news content that limits the acquisition of factual knowledge.

Based on this, it can be expected that the effects of media on political knowledge should differ across media types, with the most pronounced effects occurring from using traditional news media and weaker or nonexistent effects arising from using social media and messaging services.

3.3 Results

We used a multilevel structural equation model (SEM) to explore the relationships between media use as the independent variable and political knowledge as a latent dependent variable. In the SEM, we control for sociodemographic characteristics, ideology, and political interest. Since all variables are min/max-normalized, a direct comparison of effect sizes is possible.

The results show that both traditional and new media genres display effects in the expected pattern. More specifically, Figure 4 indicates that more frequent use of newspapers is positively associated with political knowledge. More specifically, individuals who indicated they read newspapers the most answered 40 percent more questions correctly than those on the low end of the scale. The same holds true for TV news use, though the effect is smaller (8 percent more knowledge for high-intensity users compared to low-intensity users). In other words, more frequent use of newspapers, as well as more frequent TV viewership for news, is associated with higher political knowledge. Overall, the relationship between the frequency of using newspapers and political knowledge is stronger than the association between TV news use and political knowledge.

When looking at the use of newer media types, that is, social media platforms and messaging services, we can observe that the effects run in the opposite direction. Using social media platforms or messaging services more frequently to get news is associated with lower levels of political knowledge. More specifically, the results show that individuals who use social media platforms the most have 21 percent lower levels of political knowledge than nonusers of social media. Similarly, savvy users of messaging services have 66 percent less political knowledge compared to nonusers. Particularly, the use of messaging services turns out to be the strongest predictor among the media genre variables.

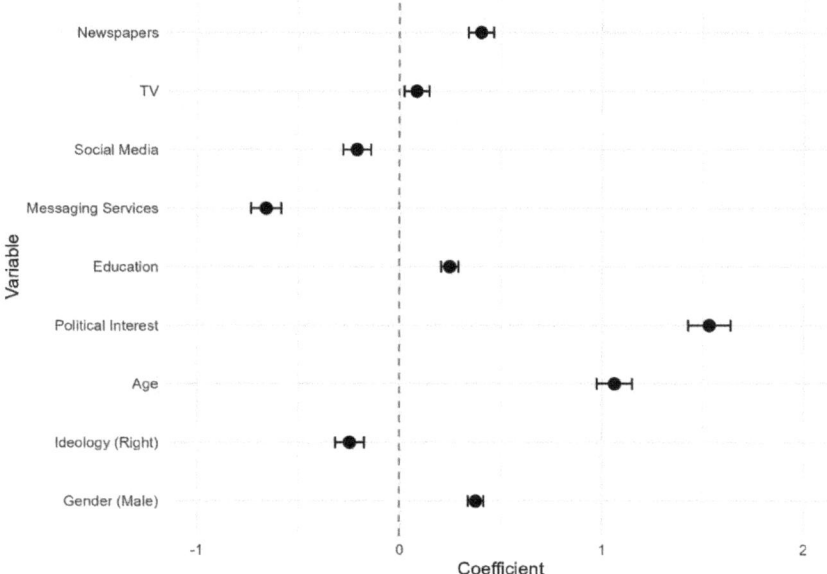

Figure 4 Coefficients for news genres and political knowledge across countries.

However, it is important to note that the effects of using different media types on political knowledge are still relatively small compared to some of our control variables (see Figure 4). For example, the results show that political interest and age play a more important role as predictors of political knowledge than media use, with higher political interest and higher age being positively associated with political knowledge. Education and ideology, in contrast, play a rather modest role, with better-educated and more left-leaning people having slightly more political knowledge than their less well-educated and right-leaning counterparts, respectively.

There may, however, be differences across groups with different education levels. Therefore, we calculated the interactions between individuals' education and the news genres. The analysis reveals a positive interaction between newspaper use and education on political knowledge ($B = 0.150$, $p = 0.024$) (see Figure 5). Since the direct effects on political knowledge are positive for both newspaper use and education, this shows that the positive relationship is stronger among individuals with higher levels of education. Among less-educated individuals, the association between newspaper use and political knowledge is weaker. There were no significant interactions between education and the other news media genres.

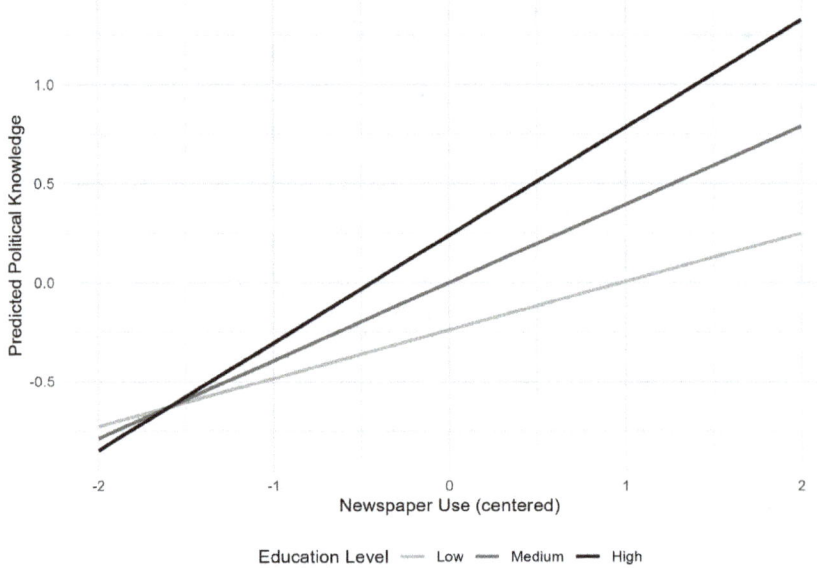

Figure 5 Interaction between newspaper use and education on political knowledge.

3.3.1 Country Comparisons

While the results discussed thus far pertain to the aggregate level, there might be differences across countries. To address this, we will next investigate how the relationship between media types and political knowledge unfolds in different countries. To this end, we estimated SEMs for each country individually, keeping the measurement and structural models exactly the same as before. The results are displayed in Figure 6, showing the coefficients for the two traditional and new media types, respectively, for each country. Before proceeding, it can be noted that the knowledge questions were arguably easier for Europeans, since some were related to European politics, which is more remote for US or Israeli citizens (see Section 2.6).

Since the overall effect of watching news on TV on knowledge was rather small, it is of interest to uncover which countries drove this effect. As Figure 5 shows, in most countries, there was no observable effect. The countries in which getting the news from TV was associated with more political knowledge were predominantly located in northwestern Europe. In Sweden, people watching news on TV the most showcased nearly twice as much (95 percent) knowledge as their low/non-TV news-watching counterparts. Significant positive effects were also found for Belgium (74 percent), Switzerland (30 percent), and Denmark (30 percent). A negative relationship between TV news use and

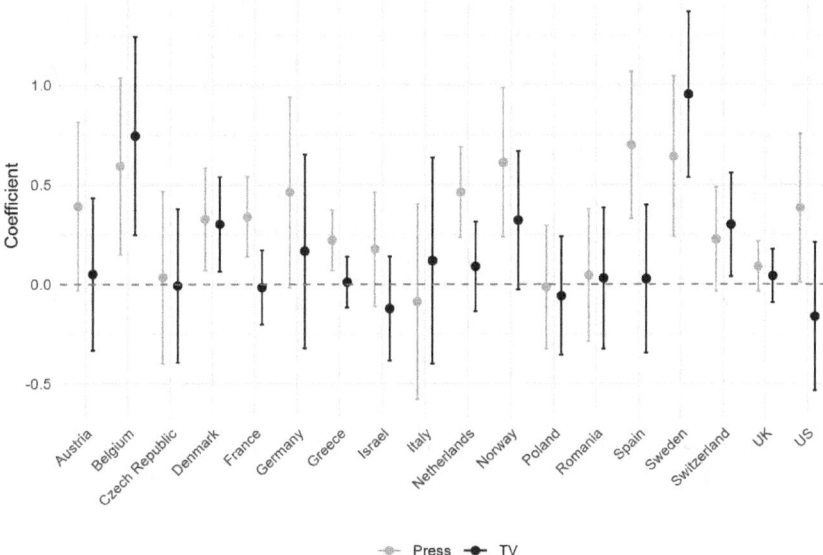

Figure 6 Coefficients for traditional news genres and political knowledge by country.

political knowledge was not found in any country, although the lowest coefficients could be observed for the two non-European countries, Israel and the US. This might indicate that television as a source of news is contributing the least to political knowledge in these countries.

In contrast, relying on newspapers for news was positively related to political knowledge in many of the countries investigated. Given the rather strong relationship shown in the multilevel model across all countries, this was to be expected. Here we find a difference in political knowledge of more than 50 percent between minimum and maximum newspaper use for Spain (70 percent), Sweden (64 percent), Norway (61 percent), and Belgium (59 percent). For people in the Netherlands (46 percent), the US (38 percent), France (34 percent), Denmark (33 percent), and Greece (22 percent), political knowledge was also higher among more frequent newspaper users. In the rest of the countries, there was no relationship between the frequency of newspaper use and political knowledge. It is important to note, though, that there is no country where newspaper use is associated with lower levels of knowledge.

Turning to the effects of using newer media types, we find that the effects of social media news use vary between countries, though they are – in line with the overall observation – either negative or nonsignificant in all of them (Figure 7). More specifically, getting news from social media platforms is associated with lower levels of political knowledge, most prominently in Norway, where those

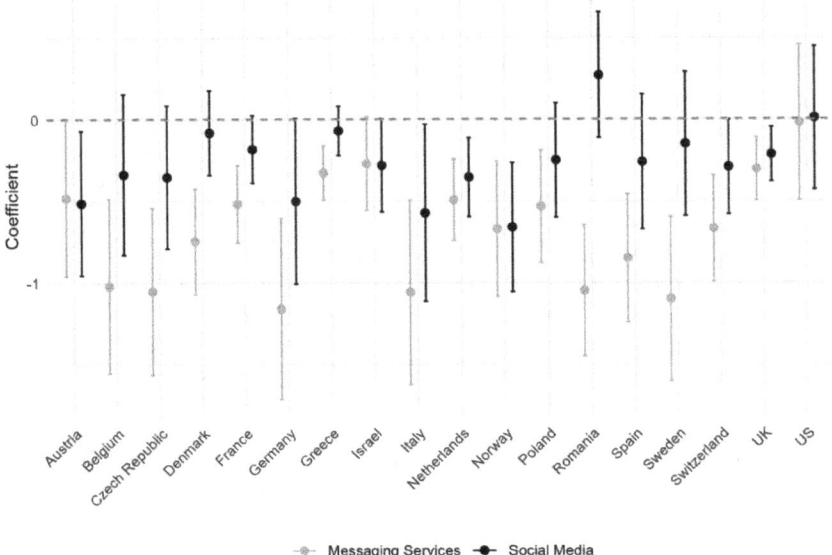

Figure 7 Coefficients for new news genres and political knowledge by country.

who indicated the highest news consumption via social media knew 66 percent less than those with the least. Similar associations are visible for Italy (57 percent), Austria (51 percent), the Netherlands (35 percent), Switzerland (29 percent), and the UK (21 percent). Although not reaching significance, Romania comes closest to being an outlier, with a positive tendency in the relationship between social media news use and political knowledge.

For news from messaging services, the negative effects are more consistent and significantly negative overall (Figure 7). However, there does not seem to be a clear geographical pattern to the strength of the effects. People who got their news from messaging services the most knew significantly less about political facts than those who indicated the lowest use. This political knowledge disadvantage amounts to more than 100 percent in Germany, Sweden, Italy, the Czech Republic, Romania, and Belgium, meaning that nonusers know more than twice as much as the savviest users of messaging services. The differences remain substantial also in the other countries, with those heavily relying on messaging apps for news having political knowledge levels 85 percent lower in Spain, 75 percent lower in Denmark, 67 percent lower in Norway and Switzerland, 53 percent lower in Poland, 52 percent lower in France, 49 percent lower in the Netherlands, 33 percent lower in Greece, and 30 percent lower in the UK. The only countries where there is no significant relationship between the use of messaging services and political knowledge are Austria, the US, and Israel.

3.4 Conclusions

In line with previous research, our findings show that more frequent use of traditional news media is associated with higher levels of political knowledge. In contrast, higher news consumption in newer media types, such as social media and messaging services, is associated with lower knowledge about political matters. For most media genres, these findings hold across different levels of education. Only with respect to newspapers do we find the positive effect to be particularly strong among people with higher education. These general findings are remarkably consistent across the countries under study. For some types of media, there is a bit more country variation. For instance, while TV use has a stronger, more variable impact depending on the country, newspapers tend to exhibit smaller and more consistent effects across contexts. Overall, this supports the assumption that more frequent news use via television and newspapers is associated with more political knowledge. There are no countries with significant effects in the opposite direction, showing that this pattern holds true regardless of different national contexts, which only seem to determine the strength of the relationships.

While social media effects tend to vary between slightly positive, zero, and slightly to more pronounced negative effects depending on the country, messaging services exhibit more consistent negative effects, albeit with considerable variability in the strength of those effects across countries. However, the overall impact of news consumption in newer media types, such as social media and messengers, on political knowledge is negative across countries.

4 News Use and Misperceptions

4.1 Introduction

While there is extensive research on the effects of using different types of media on political knowledge, in most cases, it taps into knowledge about current and – importantly – uncontroversial and uncontested issues. Typical examples might be whether people know the name of a newly elected party leader or which party put forward a certain proposal. At the same time, evidence suggests that the public debate and the media coverage often – and probably increasingly – revolve around issues where truth is contested, despite the availability of compelling and widely accessible empirical evidence (Flynn et al., 2017; Rekker, 2021; Strömbäck, Wikforss et al., 2022; Thorson, 2024b; Young, 2023). This raises the question what the relationship is between the use of different types of media and beliefs or perceptions related to contested issues. To the extent that people have perceptions that go against the scientific consensus or the best available evidence, we consider them as misinformed or holding misperceptions.

4.2 Traditional and New Media Genres and Misperceptions

The notion that public debate and media coverage increasingly focus on issues that are contested, despite widely available empirical evidence, is probably a quite universal phenomenon resulting from the emergence of high-choice media environments and increasingly fragmented information consumption. As political polarization increases, people typically disagree not only about interpreting facts but about the facts themselves (Peterson & Iyengar, 2021; Rekker, 2021; Štětka & Mihelj, 2024). Such issues can be classified as contested issues, defined as issues where there are conflicts regarding what's true. One well-known example is anthropogenic climate change, where people, and in many countries also politicians, hold polarizing views despite overwhelming scientific evidence. Other examples include the side-effects of HPV and corona-vaccines or the outcome of the 2020 US presidential election. In such cases, characterized by *epistemic or factual belief polarization*, the problem is not that some people are *uninformed*. The problem is that many people are *misinformed* and hold misperceptions, defined as perceptions that do not correspond to the best available evidence (Flynn et al., 2017; Rekker, 2021; Thorson, 2024b).

In such cases, the linkage between media use and learning may look very different compared to learning about uncontested issues (Damstra et al., 2023). On the one hand, following the news should make people more aware of scientific and other types of evidence, which should contribute to learning facts and counteract misperceptions. On the other hand, politically motivated reasoning and confirmation bias (Kunda, 1990; Lodge & Taber, 2013; Nickerson, 1998) might make people highly reluctant to change their perceptions, even if they become aware of evidence challenging those perceptions (Flynn et al., 2017; Glüer & Wikforss, 2022; 2022; Young, 2023). This holds in particular when certain beliefs have become part of people's identities and are tied to their partisan belonging (Kahan, 2016; Lodge & Taber, 2013; Shehata & Strömbäck, 2020). More specifically, partisan motivated reasoning and confirmation bias might influence what media people use, as well as what they learn and how they interpret information that they come across. In this study, we will focus on the latter aspect.

With respect to traditional news media in established democracies, they are highly influenced by the journalistic norm that any information they publish should be verified and correspond to reality (Hanitzsch et al., 2011; Kovach & Rosenstiel, 2021). Although mistakes certainly occur, their raison d'être is to provide verified and truthful information that people can rely on. If news use generally helps people learn about politics and current events, it thus seems logical that using traditional news media could increase resilience to misinformation (Humprecht et al., 2020). By reporting on or debunking false or misleading information, the news media could potentially make people more aware and thereby decrease beliefs in false and misleading information (Altay et al., 2024; Vaccari et al., 2023; Walter et al., 2020).

At the same time, research suggests that much misinformation is actually disseminated through traditional news media. Even if traditional news media strive to debunk false and misleading information, by the mere act of reporting such information, they help disseminate it to wider audiences (Thorson, 2024a; Tsfati et al., 2020). Also important is that the news media, in their efforts to be detached and impartial, often fall into the trap of "he said, she said" and false equivalence without checking the accuracy of the information provided by different news sources (Thorson, 2024a). This tendency is particularly evident when high-profile and powerful actors, such as politicians, spread false and misleading information, as is illustrated by the case of Donald Trump. Even so, on balance, the use of traditional news media should be associated with lower levels of misperceptions. Support for that has also been found in some studies (Altay et al., 2024; Damstra et al., 2023; Vliegenthart et al., 2023).

With respect to social media platforms, the situation is very different. On these channels, there are no gatekeepers, and the prevalence of false and misleading information is generally much higher, either because they are used strategically to spread false and misleading information or because people are sharing false and misleading information that they think is true (Chadwick et al., 2022; Lecheler & Egelhofer, 2022; Strömbäck, Boomgaarden et al., 2022; Theocharis et al., 2023). Therefore, users are more likely to be exposed to misinformation on social media platforms, with little exposure to fact checking or counter information, which are more common in traditional journalistic reports. This fast proliferation of false information on digital platforms is also driven by the lack of individuals' motivation to verify suspected falsehoods, seek additional information, and reach an accurate conclusion (Pennycook & Rand, 2019). Such attempts are highly demanding in contemporary digital environment, which is abundant with information, and might even lead to exposure to low quality information sources that further foster misperceptions (Aslett et al., 2024).

Confirmation bias and politically motivated selective exposure may, in conjunction with algorithms, also lead some people to seek out and trust attitude-consistent information on social media and messaging services (Flaxman et al., 2016; Hart et al., 2009; Pariser, 2011; Shin & Thorson, 2017), even if such information may be false and misleading. This holds in particular as attitude-consistent information, in general, is perceived as more trustworthy. At the same time, evidence suggests that most people are also exposed to cross-cutting information on social media (Bakshy et al., 2015; Garrett & Stroud, 2014; Zoizner et al., 2022) and that rather few live in isolated "echo chambers" (Fletcher et al., 2021; Guess, 2021). Exactly what people are exposed to in their social media feeds and through messaging services also differs widely, implying that uniform effects are less likely. Even so, it is reasonable to expect that the use of social media and messaging services will be associated with more misperceptions than the use of traditional news media.

4.3 Results

Turning to the analysis and results, we expect that people who rely more on traditional news media outlets, such as TV and newspapers, will have fewer misperceptions. In contrast, besides a negative relationship between newer media outlets and political knowledge, we expect that higher use of social media and messaging services for political information will be associated with higher levels of misperceptions. To test these assumptions, we again applied a multilevel SEM to analyze these relationships across countries, in this case with misperceptions as a latent variable. The index consists of the items described in Section 2.2.3

At first glance, the results show that the pattern of the coefficients for misperceptions (Figure 8) mirrors the results related to political knowledge (Section 3, Figure 4), indicating opposite effects. Looking at traditional news media, both newspaper and TV use are negatively related to misperceptions,

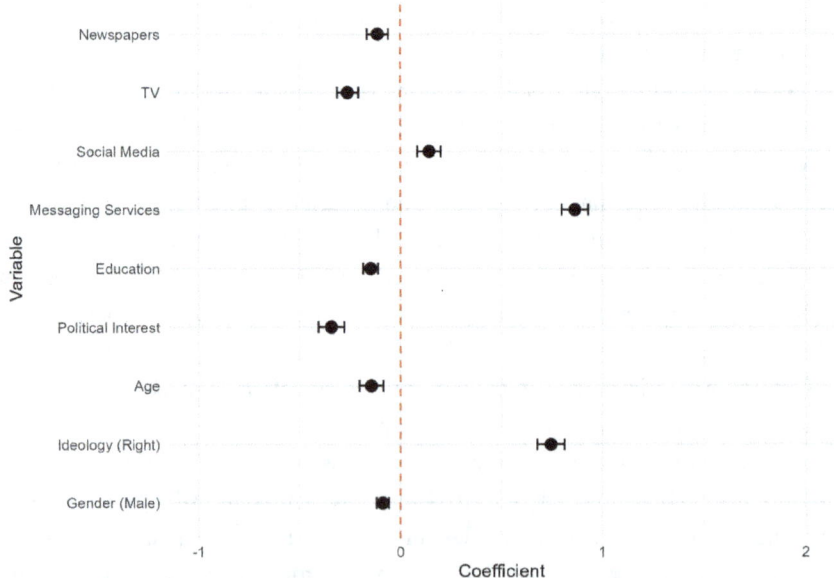

Figure 8 Coefficients for misperceptions across countries.

although TV news seems to protect more effectively from holding misperceptions than newspapers, which have a rather small effect. More specifically, the results show that individuals who watch TV news most frequently hold fewer misperceptions by 26 percent (11 percent for newspapers) compared to people hardly using TV news. Unlike traditional news outlets, the frequency of use of both social media platforms and messaging services goes hand in hand with higher levels of misperceptions. Relative to low social media use, maximum reliance on social media news supply is related to 14 percent more misperceptions, while heavy users of messaging service news hold 86 percent more misperceptions than those who do not get their news from there.

In addition, the findings also show that individuals with right-wing political attitudes and low levels of education are more likely to hold misperceptions (by 75 and 15 percent, respectively). Being male and more interested in politics is associated with fewer false beliefs (by 9 percent and 34 percent, respectively). This is also the case for older individuals (by 15 percent).

Just as with knowledge, we can expect that educational level might influence the relationship between media use and misperceptions. To investigate this, we calculated the interaction effects of news use and education. In short, the results showed a moderating effect of education on the relationship between TV news use and misperceptions ($B = 0.163$, $p = 0.004$). More specifically, the negative association between TV news use and misperceptions is particularly pronounced among individuals with lower education levels, while it weakens for those with medium education and is minimal among the highly educated, indicating a protective effect that decreases with higher education levels (see Figure 9). This seems to suggest that a more frequent use of TV news has a leveling effect, decreasing the gap in misperceptions among people with different levels of education. However, it might also reflect that people with lower education rely more heavily on TV news as a source of (credible) information than people with higher education, who might rely on a broader information diet.

4.3.1 Country Comparisons

Similar to the findings related to political knowledge, there may, however, be differences across countries. Next, we will, therefore, examine how these patterns manifest in different country contexts. Toward that end, we compare coefficients from individual SEMs conducted in each country separately.

The results in Figure 10 show that in many, albeit not all, countries, there is a clear negative relationship between TV news viewership and holding misperceptions. More specifically, individuals who rely heavily on TV news are less prone to hold misperceptions (compared to those who hardly use the medium) in Germany

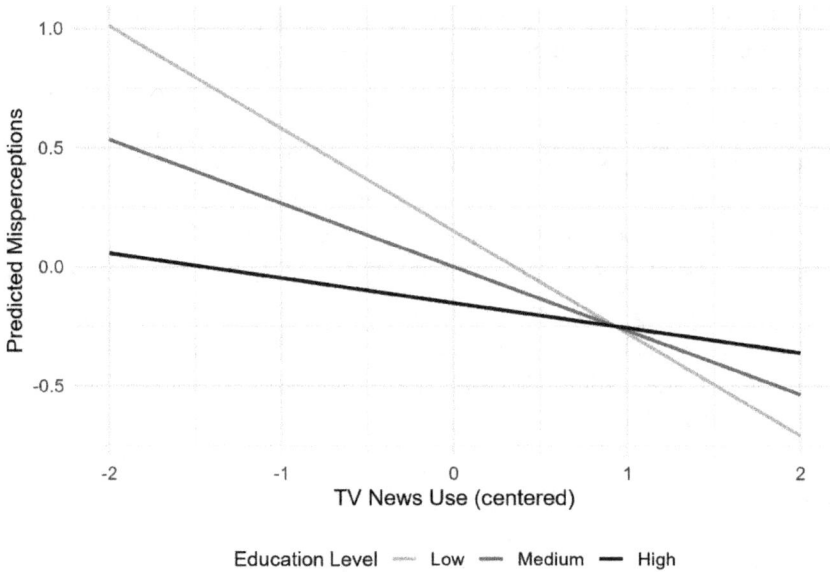

Figure 9 Interaction between TV news use and education on misperceptions.

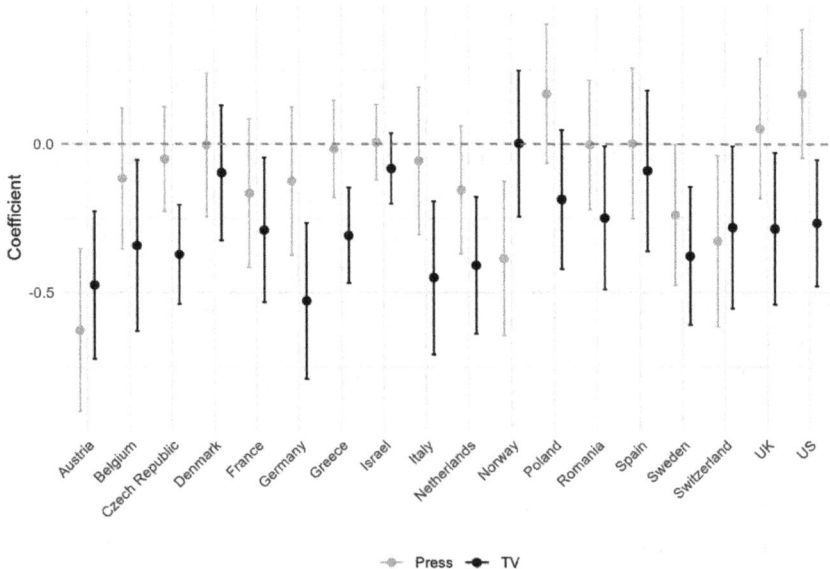

Figure 10 Coefficients for traditional news sources and misperceptions, categorized by country.

(by 53 percent), Austria (47 percent), Italy (45 percent), the Netherlands (41 percent), Sweden (38 percent), the Czech Republic (37 percent), Belgium (34 percent), Greece (31 percent), France (29 percent), the UK (28 percent), Switzerland

(28 percent), the US (27 percent), and Romania (25 percent). It is also important to note that there is no effect in the opposite direction in any of the countries.

In comparison to TV, most of the coefficients for newspaper use cluster around zero. This suggests that the overall negative effect on misperceptions found in the multilevel SEM model is driven by only a few countries. Here, the results show that this effect is driven by Austria, Norway, Switzerland, and Sweden. More specifically, people who get news from newspapers with the highest frequency exhibit a lower level of misperceptions by 63 percent in Austria, 38 percent in Norway, 33 percent in Switzerland, and 24 percent in Sweden compared to individuals who never or very seldom get news from newspapers. In all the other countries, there are no significant associations between newspaper news use and misperceptions.

Turning to the effects of using social media platforms and messaging services in individual countries, the results in Figure 11 show some variation for both these and their relationships with levels of misperceptions. Although the overall pattern suggests that the use of social media platforms is associated with more misperceptions, many coefficients are close to zero.

That said, the results show a higher level of misperceptions for those getting their news from social media several times a day – 32 percent in Switzerland and 28 percent in Italy – compared to individuals who never get news from

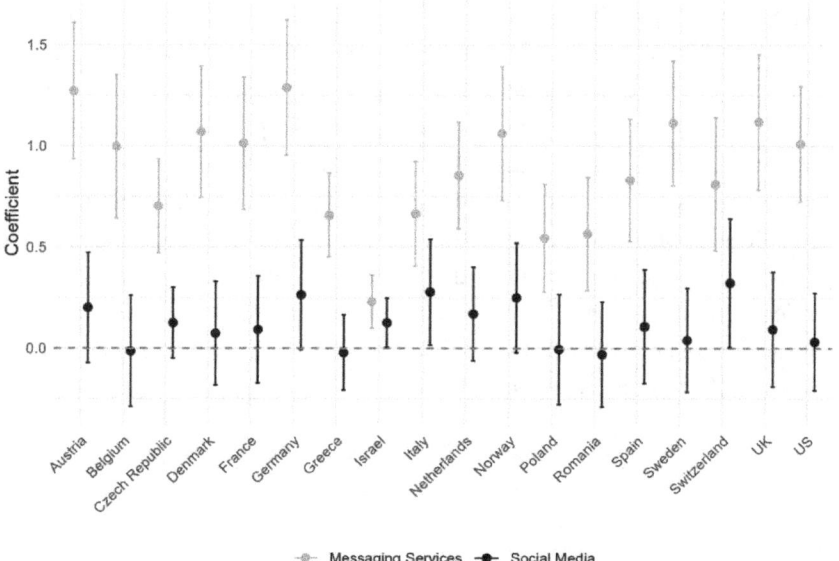

Figure 11 Coefficients for new news genres and misperceptions by country.

social media. Importantly, there is not a single country where the use of social media platforms is associated with lower levels of misperceptions.

Getting news via messaging services, however, proves to be much more consistently associated with misperceptions, as the relationship is positive and significant for every single country. It is also stronger than the effect of using social media platforms in all cases. More specifically, in Austria and Germany, people who used messenger services most frequently held almost 130 percent more misperceptions than those who indicated no or very low use. Additionally, with maximum messenger use, misperceptions more than doubled in the UK, Sweden, Denmark, Norway, France, and the US. In Israel, where the link was the weakest, there was still an increase in misperceptions of 23 percent.

4.4 Conclusions

To what extent is the frequency of use of different types of media a catalyst for misperceptions? While our findings show some variation across countries, an overall pattern is that, in general, using traditional news media seems to limit misperceptions related to contested issues, while the use of newer media, in contrast, is associated with higher levels of misperceptions. This holds, in particular, for the use of message services.

Regarding the use of traditional news media, the relationship with TV is particularly consistent. The assumption that the more individuals consume TV news, the less likely they are to hold misperceptions holds true for nearly all countries, while the effects of newspapers are more diverse and oftentimes not observable. The results also show that lower-educated people benefit most from following TV news in acquiring knowledge on contested issues and limiting misbeliefs. In contrast, the reliance on social media platforms and messaging services for political information seems to play a role in the prevalence of misperceptions. The impact of getting news from social media platforms is, however, not consistent, suggesting that the relationship is more complex and dependent on country and/or individual contexts. Getting news from messaging services, on the other hand, was visibly an important factor in holding misbeliefs across all countries. In the final section, we will further elaborate on this negative effect of messaging services.

5 The Importance of Different Types of TV News and Newspapers

5.1 Introduction

So far, we have focused on how exposure to different types of media may have different effects on knowledge and misperceptions. In this section, we will extend these analyses by differentiating between different types of broadcast news and newspapers. Previous studies have mainly dealt with two distinctions related to traditional media and knowledge: public versus commercial TV broadcasting and broadsheet or upmarket newspapers versus popular or mass-market newspapers. Both distinctions have a similar underlying rationale related to the audience they aim for and the content they provide. On the one hand, public broadcasting and upmarket newspapers are typically more aimed at an audience interested in politics and society and are therefore expected to provide more extensive coverage related to politics and society. Commercial broadcasters and popular tabloids or mass-market newspapers, on the other hand, typically aim for a much broader audience and therefore tend to provide less hard news about politics and society or mix their political content with more infotainment elements. To take this into account, we will also explore how these different mainstream media types are associated with people's political knowledge and (mis)perceptions. In the next part, we will discuss previous research related to the two distinctions between public versus commercial broadcasting and upmarket (broadsheets) versus mass-market (popular) newspapers.

5.2 Public Service versus Commercial Broadcasting and Upmarket versus Mass-Market Newspapers

The first important distinction is between public and commercial broadcasting. Most studies indicate that people who watch news (and current affairs) on the public broadcaster gain more knowledge compared to viewers of the commercial broadcaster (Aarts & Semetko, 2003; Cushion, 2012; Jenssen, 2009; Shehata et al., 2015; Soroka et al., 2013; Strömbäck, 2017). This is mainly related to the finding that public service TV usually offers more and higher-quality political information opportunities than commercial TV (Aalberg & Curran, 2012; Cushion, 2012; Esser et al., 2012). For instance, De Vreese and Boomgaarden (2006) showed that when media devote attention to EU politics, news consumers learn about it. Since public broadcasters devoted more attention to it than commercial stations, public broadcasting users gained more knowledge. Similarly, Fraile and Iyengar (2014) argued in their study on the European elections of 2009 that news programs aired by the public broadcaster tend to be more substantive than those of commercial channels.

Soroka and colleagues (2013) focused on country differences when comparing the relationship between political knowledge and watching the news on different types of broadcasters. Among other things, they found that public service broadcasters produce higher levels of knowledge about domestic and international affairs than commercial broadcasters in some countries (UK, Norway, Japan), while in others there is hardly any difference (Italy, South

Korea). These differences could be explained by several systemic factors, such as the share of public funding and the political independence of the public broadcaster. In particular, the last factor has been confirmed in several other studies that examined the role of news media in strengthening political knowledge (Leeson, 2008; Park & Gil de Zúñiga, 2020): for public broadcasting to have a positive effect, they need to be politically independent and not too reliant on advertising revenue. In Section 6, we will further discuss the role of press freedom to explain country variation.

The second important distinction is that between upmarket newspapers and mass-market newspapers. Here, the research is more limited, as only a few studies explicitly distinguish between the two types of newspapers. Partly, this is because the distinction in many countries is less clear-cut than in the case of broadcasters. One exception is a study by Elo and Rapeli (2010), who found that, in the Finnish case, upmarket newspapers contributed to political knowledge, while consumption of so-called tabloids had the opposite effect. The reason is that upmarket newspapers typically provide more substantive and in-depth coverage of political issues. Thereby, they allow for an understanding of the broader context of complex topics. The negative effect of mass-market newspapers on political knowledge seems more context-dependent, however (e.g., Schäfer & Schemer, 2024). For instance, Beckers et al. (2021) found in their Belgian diary study that popular newspapers, just like commercial broadcasters, contribute to knowledge about current political events. A rather widespread claim is that these more tabloid-style forms of political coverage – for example, emphasizing politicians' tactics and personalities, or emphasizing conflicts over agreements – might attract people's attention and increase recall of political information (e.g., Mutz, 2015; Soroka, 2014; Zhao & Bleske, 1998). Baum (2003) also argued that popular media might contribute to knowledge about political events and actors by attracting audiences that typically do not use upmarket news media. In particular, he suggests that less educated and politically less interested people could benefit from media outlets that provide a mixture of hard and soft news coverage. Even so, we expect that users of popular media will know less about politics compared to people using public broadcasters and upmarket newspapers, and that they will contribute more to political knowledge than mass-market media do.

Turning to the relationship with misperceptions, similar to the argument for mainstream media in general, we expect that reading upmarket newspapers and watching news on the public broadcaster will lead to lower levels of misperceptions compared to the use of more commercialized broadcasters or mass-market newspapers. An underlying reason is that false information is typically characterized by emotionality, surprise, negativity, and a great emphasis on polarization and conflicts (Allcott and Gentzkow, 2017; Lebernegg et al., 2024; Mosleh et al., 2024; Weeks, 2024). These features are considered important news values that make stories more newsworthy, especially in commercial broadcasters and mass-market newspapers (De Vreese et al., 2017). Thus, it is expected that commercialized and popular news outlets will disseminate more mis- and disinformation, potentially exposing their viewers and readers (Tsfati et al., 2020), and thus contributing to public misperceptions in the long run, even if the information is corrected in the short term (Carey et al., 2022; Nyhan et al., 2020). These expectations are in line with recent empirical evidence in the context of misinformation about COVID-19 (Altay et al., 2024). In the UK, for example, consuming the BBC for news and reading upmarket newspapers has been found to lead to more awareness of and less belief in false claims about the pandemic and vaccines.

5.3 Results

Turning to the results, beyond the overall effect of traditional news media discussed in Sections 3 and 4, we assume the relationship might be more nuanced and that the type of broadcasting and newspaper used matters. More specifically, we expect public service broadcasting and upmarket newspapers to be associated with more political knowledge, while the use of commercial broadcasting and popular newspapers might not have such a straight-forward relationship with knowledge. To analyze this effect across all countries, we replaced TV use at the media type level with the use of specific public and commercial broadcast outlets in the multilevel SEM used in the previous sections. The same substitution took place for newspapers, where instead of the overall newspaper use, we included frequency measures of upmarket and mass-market papers from each of the countries (see the Online Appendix). The other media outlets (i.e., social media platforms and messaging services) and controls remained the same.

The results in Figure 12 show that, overall, a more frequent consumption of public service broadcasting news is – in line with our expectation – indeed associated with higher levels of political knowledge. Between those who use public service broadcasting news the least and the most, there is a difference in knowledge of 64 percent. When comparing both broadcasting subtypes, we find that commercial TV news use is not only unrelated to higher levels of political knowledge but negatively associated with knowledge (a 39 percent difference between low and high users). The use of upmarket newspapers is also related to more knowledge, although the difference is smaller than that of public service broadcasting (a 44 percent difference in knowledge when the lowest and highest user groups are

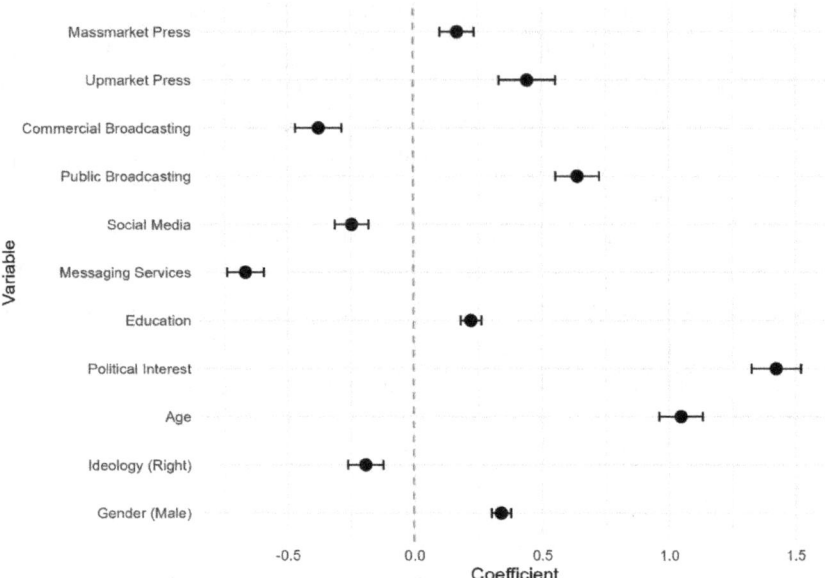

Figure 12 Coefficients for media channels and political knowledge across countries.

compared). The newspaper subtypes are both related to higher levels of political knowledge. The higher level of political knowledge is, however, less than half as pronounced with the use of mass-market newspapers (17 percent) compared to upmarket newspapers.

Again, we also calculated interaction effects of education to unveil potentially varying effects for different groups of individuals (see Figure 13). Although Section 3 showed that the positive effect of TV news use overall on political knowledge was not influenced by education levels, these analyses on types of broadcasters reveal a significant negative interaction between PBS use and education ($B = -0.221, p = 0.020$), indicating that political knowledge gains are stronger for those with lower education than for those with higher education. No significant interaction was found for commercial TV use.

The relationship between newspaper use and knowledge, on the other hand, is influenced by education. A more detailed analysis of newspaper types refines the earlier pattern. More specifically, we find a significant interaction for both upmarket ($B = 0.386, p = 0.002$) and mass-market newspaper use ($B = -0.192, p = 0.015$). While individuals with higher educational levels seem to benefit more from upmarket outlets than their lower-educated counterparts, the opposite can be said about mass-market newspapers: individuals with lower education levels gain more political knowledge, whereas there are minimal effects for the

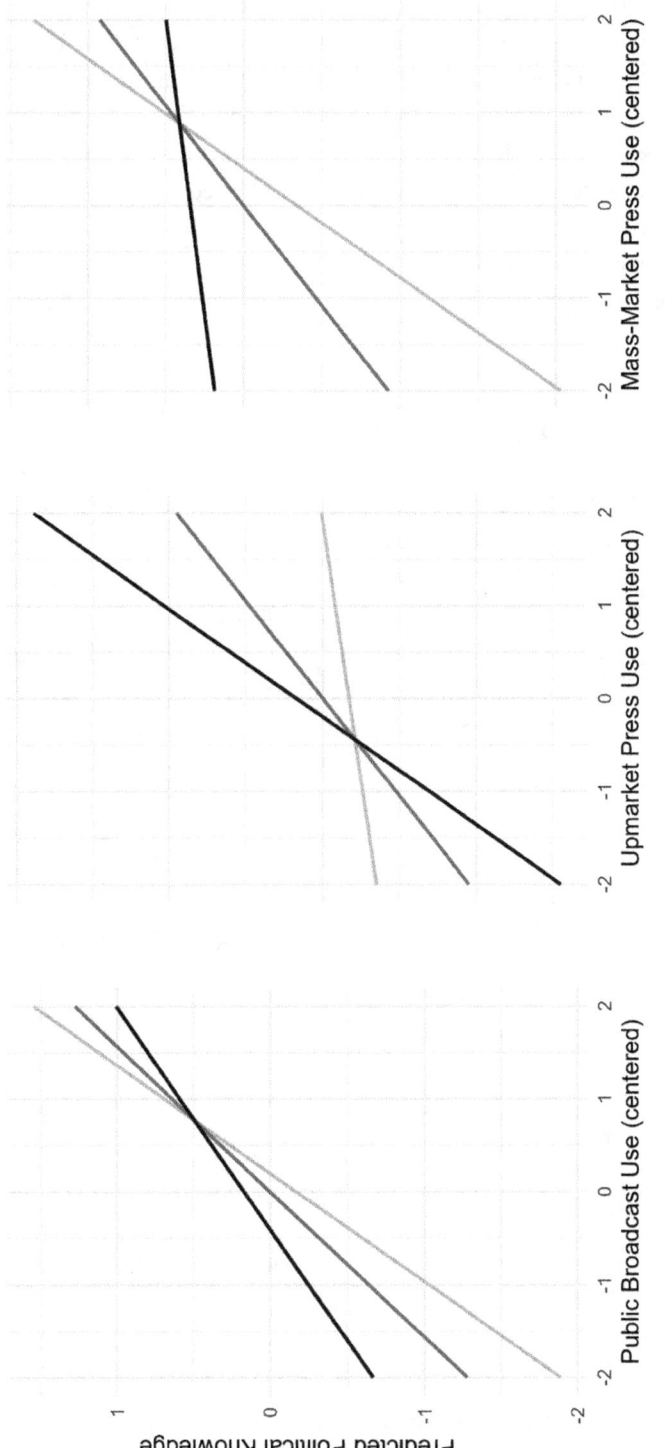

Figure 13 Interaction between news genre types and education on political knowledge.

highly educated. Taken together, these findings highlight that individual-level education not only shapes the overall benefits of news consumption for political knowledge but also moderates which types of outlets are most effective. While upmarket newspapers seem to reinforce existing knowledge advantages among the highly educated, public broadcasting and mass-market newspapers appear to offer more substantial gains for those with lower education. This suggests that more informative but also accessible news formats may help reduce knowledge gaps, whereas more demanding formats continue to privilege already advantaged groups.

5.3.1 Country Differences

While these results apply to the aggregate levels, there might be differences across countries. To take different media environments into account, we again ran SEMs, but for each country individually. First, we investigate the effects of public and commercial broadcasting in the countries under study.

In line with the previously described overall effects, the results show that in almost all countries, getting news from public service providers is associated with more knowledge of political issues (see Figure 14). The link is strongest in Sweden, Austria, and Belgium, where the highest use of news on public service channels is associated with above 1.5 times more knowledge compared to the

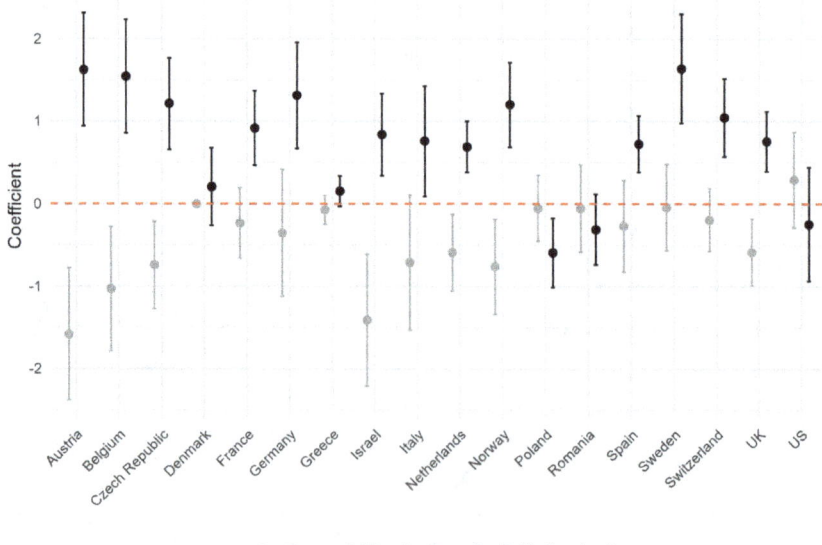

Figure 14 Coefficients for the type of broadcasting and political knowledge by country.

lowest user group. More than twice as much political knowledge between heavy and light-users was observed for Germany, the Czech Republic, Norway, and Switzerland, followed by less pronounced positive differences in France (92 percent difference), Israel (84 percent), Italy and the UK (both 76 percent), Spain (73 percent), and the Netherlands (69 percent). In Denmark and Greece, the positive relationship is not significant. However, the results also show that the relationship is negative in three countries, namely Romania, the US, and, most clearly, Poland. In the case of the US, this might be related to the low market share of the public broadcasters. Potentially, the negative correlation between knowledge and the Polish public service broadcaster can be attributed to the specific context of the country during the time of our study and the politicization of Polish broadcasting (Štětka & Mihelj, 2024). We will elaborate on the Polish case and the role of press freedom in the next section.

In contrast to using public service TV news, consuming news from commercial broadcasting channels is typically not beneficial in promoting political knowledge (Fraile & Iyengar, 2014; Soroka et al., 2013; Strömbäck, 2017). This is shown by the negative coefficient in the multilevel model. Relative to no use, intense reliance on commercial TV channels for news is associated with lower knowledge in Austria (by 158 percent), Israel (141 percent), Belgium (103 percent), Norway (76 percent), the Czech Republic (74 percent), the Netherlands (59 percent), and the UK (58 percent). In the other countries, we did not find any significant relationships.

The following analysis focuses on the effects of using different types of newspapers, and more specifically, upmarket and mass-market newspapers. As expected, we find much more variation between countries with respect to this distinction.

With respect to the use of upmarket newspapers, the overall pattern is a positive relationship with political knowledge. Looking at countries individually, it becomes apparent, however, that this effect is largely driven by a few countries. By far the strongest link between the use of upmarket newspapers and higher levels of political knowledge can be observed in the Czech Republic, where political knowledge for individuals with the highest level of use was four times higher than the political knowledge of nonusers. Other countries with a significant positive relationship are the US (difference in knowledge of 148 percent), Spain (131 percent), Germany (101 percent), Poland (94 percent), Romania (82 percent), and the UK (58 percent). In the remaining countries, the results show null effects, with the exception of Belgium, where the most frequent use of upmarket newspapers is related to lower knowledge compared to nonusers.

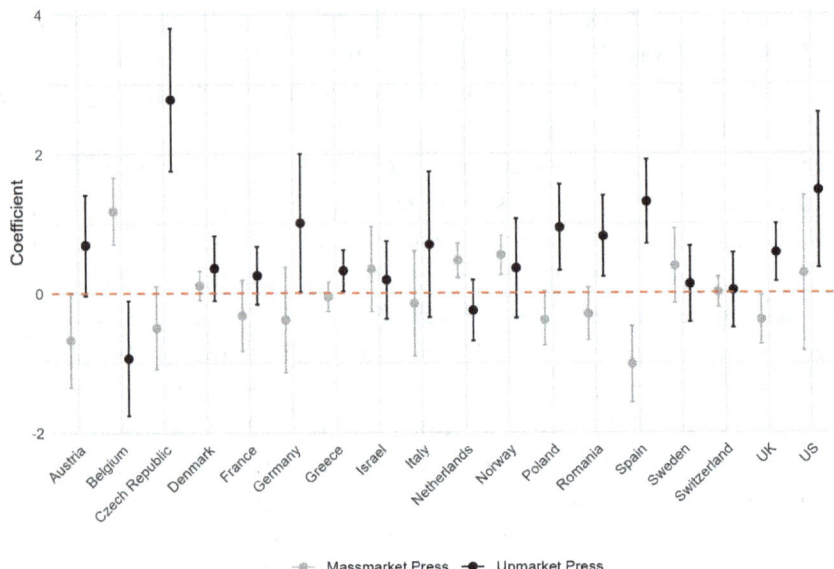

Figure 15 Coefficients for press and political knowledge by country.

The results for mass-market newspapers are even more diverse (see Figure 15). Here, we find countries in which more exposure to news from these newspapers is associated with more political knowledge, but also one(s) where the opposite scenario is the case. In the former category, we can place Belgium (118 percent more political knowledge for mass-market newspaper readers), Norway (54 percent), and the Netherlands (47 percent). This stands in contrast to the use of upmarket newspapers in countries that did not yield knowledge-increasing effects. In Spain, individuals who read mass-market newspapers displayed lower levels of political knowledge by 102 percent, and a similar effect was found for the UK (39 percent). In the other countries, the effects were not significant.

5.3.2 Misperceptions

Turning to the effects of using different types of traditional news media on misperceptions, we expect the roles of using different types of broadcasting and press to be reversed. While getting news from public service broadcasting providers and upmarket newspapers is likely to hinder misperceptions, we do not expect commercial broadcasts and mass-market newspapers to have the same effect. The results of the multilevel SEM show that while most assumptions hold true, there are findings that do not match our expectations (Figure 16). As expected, the results show that using public service broadcasting as a source of information is most often related to lower levels of misperceptions – by almost

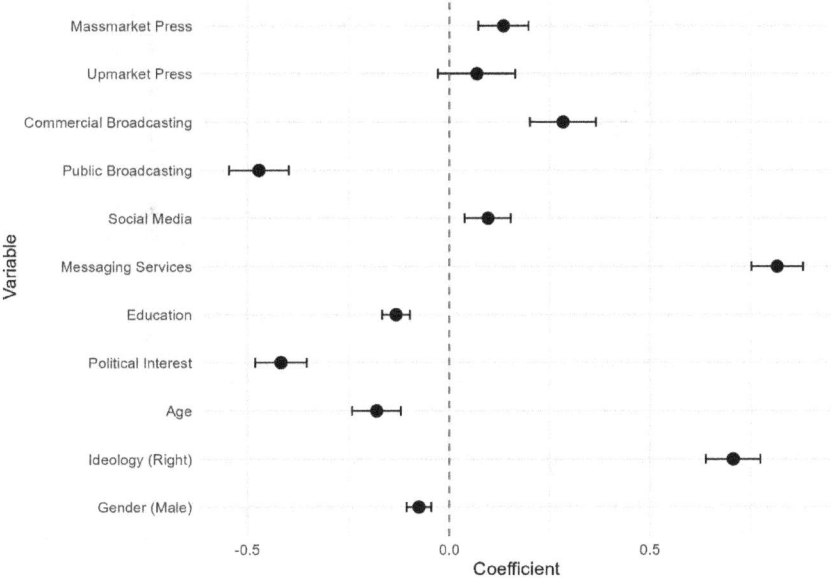

Figure 16 Coefficients for mainstream media types and misperceptions across countries.

50 percent compared to nonusers. Inconsistent with our expectations, this is, however, not the case for the use of upmarket newspapers, where we find no significant relationships. Interestingly, individuals who consume news from commercial broadcast providers the most – who were previously found to display higher levels of political knowledge – also hold 28 percent more misperceptions than nonusers. This same phenomenon can be observed for mass-market newspapers, where greater use in the overall model is not only associated with more political knowledge but also more misperceptions – by 13 percent. This supports the necessity of investigating countries individually, since there does not seem to be a clear pattern in how these news sources relate to misperceptions.

To further investigate the role of education in shaping the relationship between news consumption and misperceptions, we analyzed interaction effects for the media subtypes (see Figure 17). For public broadcasting service (PBS), we find a consistent protective effect across all education levels, with this effect becoming stronger as education increases ($B = -0.194$, $p = 0.012$). The interaction effect of education and commercial broadcasting use is more complex ($B = 0.357$, $p < 0.001$): among individuals with medium and especially high education levels, misperceptions are more widespread among those with higher use, while among the lower educated, the relationship is even slightly negative, hinting at reduced misperceptions.

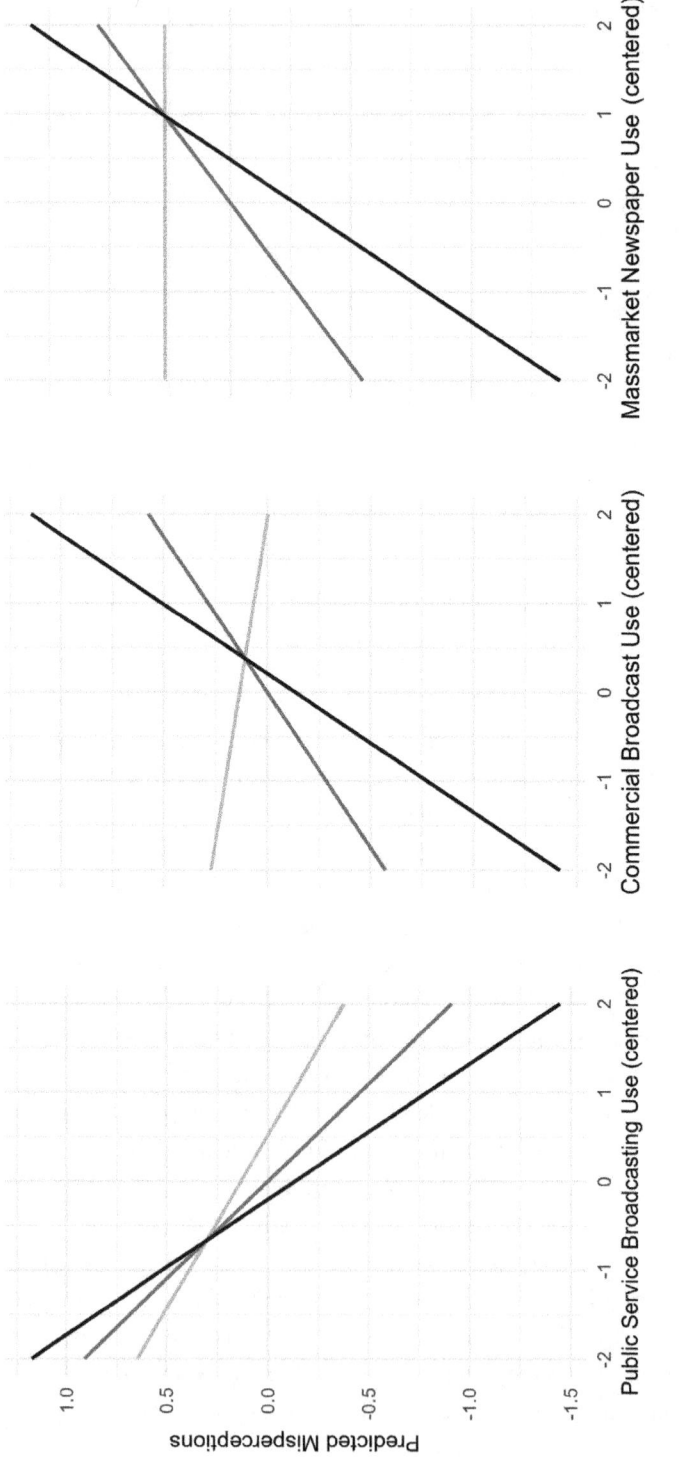

Figure 17 Interaction between news genre types and education on misperceptions.

A similar interaction pattern is observed for mass-market newspaper use ($B = 0.137, p = 0.036$), which is positively associated with misperceptions among the highly educated but not among those with lower education. Education does not affect the relationship between up-market press use and misperceptions.

Taken together, these findings nuance the results on political knowledge, where mass-market newspapers were most beneficial for lower-educated individuals. In the case of misperceptions, both commercial broadcasting and mass-market newspapers appear to be linked to higher levels of misinformation acceptance – at least among more educated individuals. This points to a two-edged sword: while mass-market and commercial formats may effectively inform individuals with lower education, they may also reinforce or even amplify misperceptions among more educated consumers, perhaps due to motivated reasoning or selective exposure. Importantly, PBS stands out as the only news source with a consistent and strengthening protective effect across education levels.

Turning to differences across countries, the results show that the relationship between using these different mainstream media types and misperceptions differs across countries, although some patterns can be identified. Consistent with the overall relationship, relying on news from public service broadcasters is associated with lower levels of misperceptions in most countries (Figure 18). This effect is especially strong in Austria (difference in misperceptions by

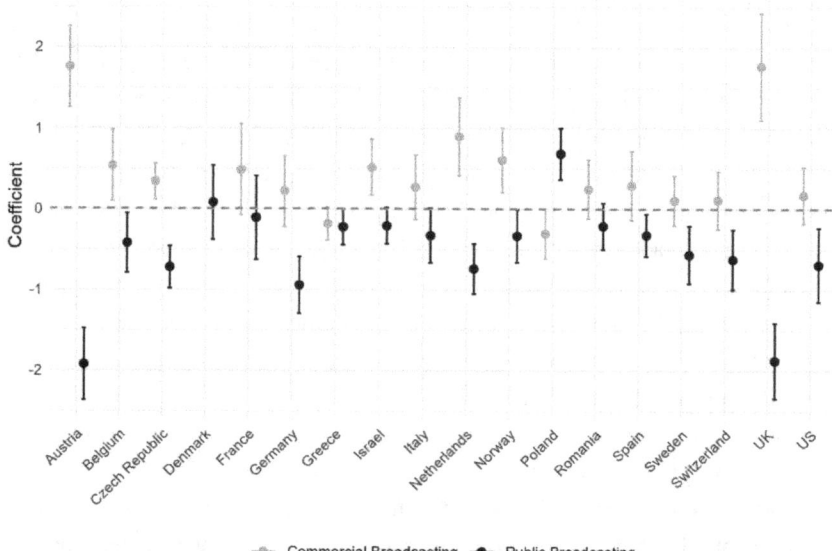

Figure 18 Coefficients for broadcasting and misperceptions by country.

192 percent when the highest and lowest user groups are compared) and the UK (187 percent). Misperceptions are also reduced with regular use of public service broadcasting news in Germany (94 percent), the Netherlands (73 percent), the Czech Republic (72 percent), the US (69 percent), Switzerland (62 percent), Sweden (56 percent), Belgium (42 percent), Norway (33 percent), and Spain (32 percent). The noteworthy exception to the overall pattern is again Poland, where people who heavily rely on public broadcasting news hold 69 percent more misperceptions than those who do not.

As is the case with political knowledge, the effects of commercial broadcasting are less straightforward. There is, however, no country where consuming news via commercial broadcasting channels is related to fewer misperceptions. In most countries, there is either no relationship or a relatively small positive one. Positive relationships are found in Austria and the UK, where those who indicate a high use of commercial broadcasting hold close to three times more misperceptions than nonusers, which mirrors the previously found protective effect of PBS broadcasting in these countries. We also found misperceptions to be more prevalent with more frequent use of commercial channels in the Netherlands (by 90 percent), Norway (61 percent), Belgium (54 percent), Israel (52 percent), and the Czech Republic (34 percent). An exception is, again, Poland, where we observe the opposite: while public broadcasting use is associated with more misperceptions, relying on the commercial counterparts is associated with fewer misperceptions by 30 percent.

Related to newspaper use, differences between up- and mass-market newspapers are not as consistent across countries (Figure 19). For most countries, there is no significant relationship between the use of upmarket newspapers and misperceptions. Only in Greece and Austria do people who regularly read upmarket newspapers hold fewer misperceptions (by 92 percent and 57 percent, respectively). For the remaining countries, there are no significant associations, except for Israel, where the most frequent use of newspapers categorized as upmarket is associated with 35 percent higher levels of misperceptions compared to nonusers.

For mass-market newspapers, we also find some variation across countries. In the majority of countries, there is no relationship with misperceptions, but we also find negative as well as positive associations. A substantially higher level of misperceptions, associated with more frequent consumption of mass-market newspapers, can be observed in Greece (by 151 percent), the US (90 percent), Spain (76 percent), the UK (69 percent), and Germany (50 percent). In the cases of Norway and Belgium, the use of mass-market newspapers is, in contrast, associated with lower levels of misperceptions (both by 37 percent).

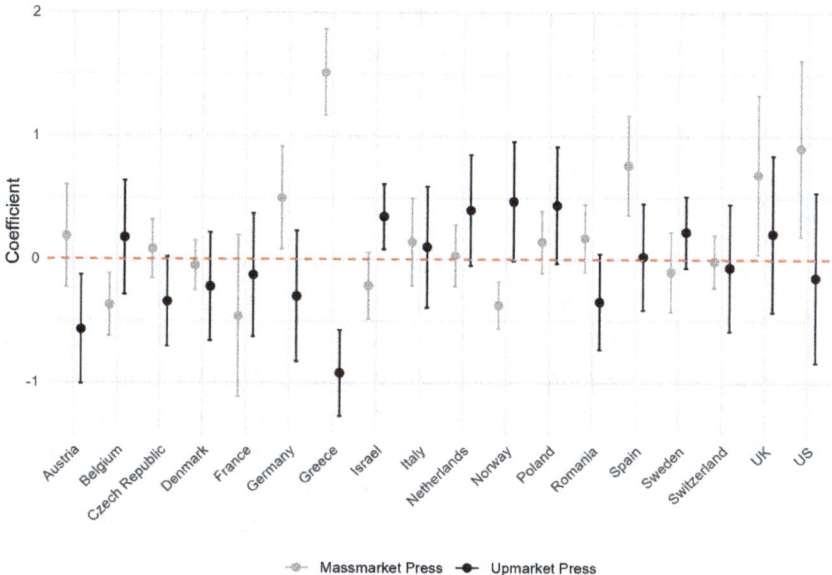

Figure 19 Coefficients for press and misperceptions by country.

5.4 Conclusions

Going beyond the relationship between mainstream media and political knowledge, in this section, we focused on the distinctions between public versus commercial broadcasting and upmarket versus mass-market newspapers. Related to public broadcasting, the effects are fairly consistent across countries. Watching news programs on the public service broadcaster is typically related to higher levels of political knowledge and lower levels of misperceptions. Moreover, public service broadcasting stands out as the only source with a consistent and strengthening protective effect across individuals' education levels. The few cases where the positive relationship between using public broadcasting and knowledge is less straightforward will be discussed in more depth later (see Section 6.5). Using commercial TV news, on the other hand, is associated with less political knowledge and more misperceptions on contested issues.

The findings for the two types of newspapers are less unequivocal. Overall, reading mass-market and upmarket newspapers is associated with a higher level of knowledge. This correlation is, however, not present consistently across countries. Furthermore, the opposite relationship is even less clear. Using newspapers hardly or not at all limits the spread of misperceptions among their readers. Again, the variation among countries is quite substantial. These mixed findings on the contribution of using different types of newspapers can probably be related to the differences between countries. In some countries, mass-market newspapers provide little hard news compared to upmarket newspapers, while in other countries, the difference is much smaller (Brekken et al., 2013).

6 Variations across Countries

6.1 Introduction

So far, we have examined how modern information environments influence people's political knowledge and misperceptions across countries, without accounting for the local conditions that may shape this relationship. However, a growing body of research has increasingly focused on understanding political communication from a comparative perspective, emphasizing how country-level factors might shape the information people consume (Esser & Hanitzsch, 2012). Such variations in media and political systems can be expected to lead to differences in how political knowledge, attitudes, and behavior are formed across different contexts (Aalberg & Curran, 2012; Castro et al., 2022; Shehata & Strömbäck, 2011; Soroka et al., 2013; Toff & Kalogeropoulos, 2020; Zoizner et al., 2022). As presented in Sections 3–5, the relationship between news use, political knowledge, and misperceptions indeed varies across different countries. For example, we found in Section 4 that while newspaper consumption is generally associated with fewer misperceptions, in some countries (Poland and the US), there is some evidence for an opposite relationship (i.e., newspaper use is associated with more misperceptions).

In this section, we will focus on the unique differences among the eighteen countries in our sample, examining how and why the relationship between news use, political knowledge, and misperceptions may depend on the local context. We approach this analysis in several stages. First, we will establish theoretical expectations, focusing in particular on countries' press freedom and education performance as key macro-level variables. Second, we will statistically analyze the role of these macro-level moderators in explaining country variations. Finally, we will focus on specific countries that consistently emerge as outliers in our main findings and offer potential explanations for these deviations.

6.2 The Role of Country-Level Factors

6.2.1 Press Freedom

Since an informed citizenry is one of the cornerstones of a healthy democracy, empirical studies have consistently focused on understanding the political information available to people within their national media environments. Scholars have identified multiple macro-level factors that shape the supply side of political information – both the amount of available information and its nature. One of the most widely studied factors is the commercialization of local media markets. News journalism in more commercialized media systems, such as that of the US, is often more dramatized, sensational, negative, and soft, in contrast to media systems dominated by strong public service broadcasters, where hard news is more prevalent (e.g., De Vreese et al., 2017). Such disparities in the availability of substantive and hard news can directly affect people's knowledge of politics and society (Aalberg & Curran, 2012; Soroka et al., 2013).

Another important macro-level factor influencing what people learn from the news is press freedom, which refers to the degree of independence that private journalistic actors have from state intervention. Press freedom, along with the strength and independence of public broadcasting, is hence considered a central indicator that differentiates media systems and the political information they provide (Hallin & Mancini, 2004; Humprecht et al., 2020; Štětka & Mihelj, 2024). Normatively, press freedom is seen as a democratic ideal, allowing journalists to fulfill their role as watchdogs and providing people with uncensored, diverse perspectives. Higher levels of press freedom not only enhance pluralism in news coverage but are also linked to more context in reporting, thereby aiding a better understanding of political events (Salgado et al., 2017). Equally important is that press freedom allows for more investigative journalism and journalistic criticism of political elites, as political elites have less control over news outlets under conditions of greater press freedom (Besley & Prat, 2006).

6.2.2 Countries' Education Performance

As elaborated in previous sections, education plays a central role in equipping citizens with the skills needed to learn from high-quality political information and resist misinformation. While we previously focused on supply-side factors, specifically levels of press freedom, countries' education performance reflects the demand side. It shapes what citizens are able and willing to seek out, process, and retain when encountering political content.

At the macro level, national education performance reflects the overall and aggregated quality of citizens' cognitive skills, such as reading comprehension or critical thinking. Theoretically, people in countries with higher educational performance are likely to be better prepared to navigate complex political information environments, critically evaluate the credibility of sources, and apply more sophisticated reasoning when forming opinions on news content (Karlsen et al., 2020; Liu & Eveland, 2005). In such contexts, news use may translate more effectively into political learning, and exposure to misinformation may be less likely to result in belief in falsehoods.

6.2.3 News Use and Political Knowledge: A Comparative Perspective

The impact of press freedom on the availability and quality of political information in a country may influence what people learn from national news sources, both directly and indirectly. For example, comparative studies have demonstrated that people living in countries with higher press freedom are generally more knowledgeable about political issues (Leeson, 2008; Park & Gil de Zúñiga, 2020; Schoonvelde, 2014). In such information-rich environments, people are routinely exposed to uncensored, diverse, and relevant information about substantive topics and policy issues, which positively affects their understanding of both day-to-day political events and fundamental institutional arrangements.

We expect this overall positive impact of press freedom on political knowledge to be particularly pronounced when people consume news from outlets that already provide, relatively speaking, high-quality information. In other words, the knowledge gains from consuming traditional news outlets, specifically public service broadcasting and upmarket newspapers, as discussed in earlier sections, should be even more significant in countries with higher levels of press freedom. Conversely, since press freedom generally improves the quality of information across the entire national media market, we expect the negative consequences of commercialized broadcasters and mass-market press for political knowledge to be mitigated in systems with greater press freedom.

We will also examine how press freedom may moderate the relationship between political knowledge and news consumption on social media platforms and messaging services. In countries with limited press freedom and weaker democratic institutions, where government constraints affect traditional media channels, people may turn to a variety of other information sources to compensate for these restrictions (Štětka & Mihelj, 2024; Szostek, 2018b; Zoizner et al., 2022). In such contexts, digital platforms such as social media and messaging services may function as both alternative and complementary tools for accessing political information, as they are harder for political elites to control (Koçak & Kıbrıs, 2023; Park & Gil de Zúñiga, 2020; Štětka & Mihelj, 2024; Szostek, 2018a). Therefore, while we originally expected weak or nonexistent effects of news use from social media and messaging services on political knowledge in general and across countries, we anticipate at least some knowledge gains from these platforms in countries with low press freedom. In these contexts, newer digital media can serve as alternative sources for political knowledge, as they enable political information to circulate without official restrictions or censorship.

Turning to the role of national education levels, we expect that citizens in countries with higher education performance will be better equipped to gain knowledge from exposure to political news across outlets and platforms. Thus, the knowledge gains obtained from traditional media, and specifically from public service broadcasters and upmarket newspapers, will be more substantial in countries with higher education performance. At the same time, we are more cautious in formulating expectations about moderation effects in the relationship between political knowledge and the consumption of news from commercialized broadcasters and the mass-market press.

Although we initially expected weaker relationships between political knowledge and news use from digital platforms, stronger knowledge gains may emerge in countries with higher national education performance. In these contexts, citizens are more likely to possess cognitive skills, such as critical thinking and information filtering, needed to extract relevant information even from lower-quality digital information environments.

6.2.4 News Use and Misperceptions: A Comparative Perspective

While the question of how social media and messaging services contribute to the spread of misperceptions has been widely studied, less attention has been given to empirically testing this issue from a comparative perspective. Globally, people report regularly encountering misinformation from both traditional and social media (Newman et al., 2018). Some attempts have been made to identify country-level factors that shape public resilience to false information. Among others, lower levels of polarization and strong public service have been identified as some important mitigators of misperceptions (Benkler et al., 2018; Humprecht, 2019; Humprecht et al., 2020). For example, lower polarization reduces the emergence of misinformation as well as the likelihood of believing and spreading it (Weeks, 2024; Young, 2023). More recent comparative studies have examined people' ability to discern between true and false claims and their beliefs in conspiracy theories across multiple countries (Gehle et al., 2024; Zilinsky et al., 2024), though they have not found consistent evidence of systematic country-level moderation.

While these and other studies offer valuable insights into the extent to which people in different countries may be exposed to false information, there is less understanding of the specific country-level factors that shape the relationship between news use and the formation of misperceptions. As in previous sections, we first focus on press freedom, which affects the availability and quality of political information within a given political context. We expect that the benefits of traditional news media, especially public service broadcasters and upmarket newspapers, in reducing misperceptions will be more pronounced in countries with high press freedom. In these contexts, public service broadcasters and upmarket newspapers have the freedom and are, to at least some extent, expected to prioritize accuracy and fact-checking in their reporting, provide broader context, and offer in-depth analyses, even if it means sacrificing immediacy (De Vreese et al., 2017; Jastrzebski & Willnat, 2023). These practices are key to enhancing people's ability to distinguish between true and false information and are expected to be more prominent in countries with higher press freedom.

In parallel, since higher press freedom typically improves the overall quality of political information across all national media, this may mitigate the potential spread of misinformation by commercialized news media. Their emphasis on simplicity, conflict, and emotion – characteristics often associated with false information (Allcott & Gentzkow, 2017; Lebernegg et al., 2024; Mosleh et al., 2024; Tsfati et al., 2020) – can thus be expected to be less dominant in media environments with higher-quality political information. Therefore, we anticipate that the negative impact of getting news from commercialized broadcasters and mass-market press on misperceptions will be weaker in countries with high press freedom.

Finally, we also explore whether press freedom moderates the relationship between misperceptions and the use of newer digital platforms. In countries with lower levels of press freedom, people can choose to supplement traditional news media with social media and messaging services for political information, given that traditional news sources are often less reliable or politically biased in such contexts (see also Gehle et al., 2024; Szostek, 2018a). This increased reliance on social media – where misinformation spreads more easily – combined with the less rigorous reporting standards of traditional media, may create a reinforcing cycle that amplifies misperceptions. In contrast, in countries with higher press freedom, the spread of false information on digital platforms might be mitigated by more accurate and factual reporting from professional journalists (Vaccari et al., 2023). In other words, the link between misperceptions and news use via social media and messaging services is expected to be stronger in countries with lower levels of press freedom.

Turning to the moderating role of national education performance, we expect that in countries with higher education performance, citizens are more equipped with relevant skills to identify and resist false claims, which leads to several implications. First, the corrective benefits of traditional news use, especially from public service broadcasters and upmarket newspapers, are likely to be stronger in highly educated societies, as citizens are better able to process and retain fact-based information. Second, higher national education performance may help mitigate the influence of more commercialized and popular media sources, which often emphasize sensationalist or emotionally charged content that can contribute to misperceptions. Third, citizens in such contexts are also more likely to discern between reliable and misleading content on digital platforms, reducing the potential harm of exposure to misinformation in digital online environments.

6.3 Results

Turning to the analyses, we relied on two measurements for assessing the level of press freedom and education performance across the eighteen countries in our sample. To measure press freedom, we used the 2022 World Press Freedom Index, developed by Reporters without Borders. This comparative index taps journalists' level of freedom across 180 countries and regions, and it is based on experts' assessments of several categories (e.g., level of pluralism, media independence, and the safety of local journalists). Higher values indicate greater press freedom for a given country. As shown in Figure 20, the distribution of press freedom in our sample indicates considerable variation, with scores ranging from 55.5 in Greece (ranked 108th in the world) to 92.6 in Norway (ranked 1st in the world). Since we focus on Western democracies, most countries fall within the moderate to high range of press freedom, with the Scandinavian countries – such as Sweden, Denmark, and Norway – achieving the highest levels. In contrast, most Southern and East European countries score

Figure 20 Press freedom and national education performance across the eighteen countries in the sample.

lower, with five countries exhibiting scores below 70 (Greece, Israel, Poland, Italy, and Romania). The US has experienced a steady decline in its press freedom scores in recent years, driven by decreasing trust in the media, political targeting of the news media, rising threats and hostility toward journalists, and other contributing factors (Albrecht, 2023; Carlson et al., 2021; Maniou, 2023; Reporters without Borders, 2024).

We measured countries' education performance using the 2022 PISA reading scores, which serve as an indicator of the overall quality of national education systems (OECD, 2023). As shown in Figure 20, there is a moderate correlation between countries' press freedom scores and their education scores ($r = 0.44$, $p < 0.001$). Education scores range from 428 in Romania (ranked 45th out of 81 participating countries in PISA 2022) to 504 in the US (ranked 9th out of 81). Most countries in our sample perform above the OECD average score of 476, with 12 out of 18 scoring above this average.

To explore whether and how the relationship between news use, political knowledge, and misperceptions is contingent on press freedom and countries' education performance, we used interactions. As in the previous sections, we employed multi-level SEMs to account for the nested structure of the data. To ease the interpretation of conditional main effects, we grand-mean-centered the independent variables that formed the interaction term.

Following the structure of the earlier sections, we begin by investigating the interaction between news use and macro-level moderators on political knowledge and misperceptions at the media type level (newspapers, TV, social media, and messaging services). Then, we will examine the interactions between macro-level factors and reliance on different media channels for news (public service versus commercialized broadcasters, and mass-market versus upmarket press). In total, we estimated eight SEMs, with different media types or channels as predictors, political knowledge or misperceptions as outcomes, and two country-level factors as moderators. Each model included all interaction terms between one country-level moderator (either press freedom or national education performance) and the various media types or channels.

All the figures presented below show the estimated slopes at different levels of a country-level moderator. More specifically, they show (1) one standard deviation below the average of a country-level moderator in our sample, (2) the average, and (3) one standard deviation above the average. Simple slopes were calculated to explore the nature of the interaction effect, enabling an evaluation of how the relationship between news use, political knowledge, and misperceptions varies across different levels of a specific country-level moderator. In each section, we first present the results for the interactions with press freedom, followed by the interactions with countries' education performance.

6.3.1 Media Type – TV

Findings show that the positive association between TV news consumption and political knowledge becomes stronger at higher levels of press freedom. The interaction between TV news use and press freedom is positive and statistically significant ($p < 0.001$). Figure 21 (left-hand plot) shows that in countries characterized by low levels of press freedom (−1 SD), there is no significant relationship between TV news consumption and political knowledge ($b = -0.044$, $p = 0.387$). In countries with average levels of press freedom, there is also no association ($b = 0.080$, $p = 0.112$). This association becomes stronger in countries with higher levels of press freedom (+1 SD, $b = 0.203$, $p < 0.001$). In Section 3, we found that the positive effect of TV news on political knowledge was primarily driven by certain countries. Our analysis here reveals that these countries are characterized by higher levels of press freedom.

As shown in the right-hand plot of Figure 21, this pattern is different for misperceptions, as the interaction term is not statistically significant at conventional levels ($p = 0.064$). One can observe a similar negative association between TV news use and misperceptions across all levels of press freedom.

Turning to the level of education, we find no evidence of a significant interaction between TV news use and countries' educational performance for either political knowledge ($p = 0.490$) or misperceptions ($p = 0.515$).

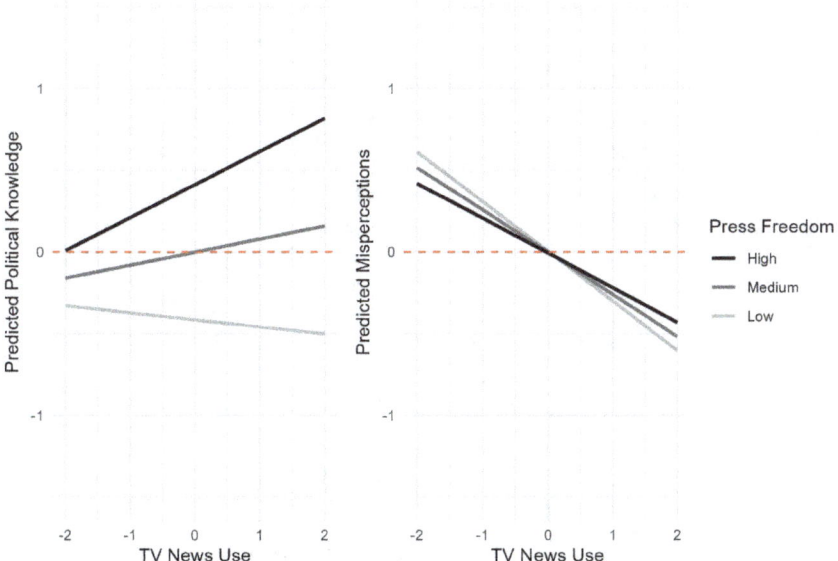

Figure 21 Interaction between TV news use and press freedom on political knowledge (left plot) and misperceptions (right plot).

6.3.2 Media Type – Newspapers

Regarding newspapers, we find evidence of a significant interaction between press freedom and newspaper use when predicting political knowledge. As is visible in Figure 22 (left plot) and confirmed by simple slopes analysis, the association between newspaper consumption and political knowledge is positive at all levels of press freedom but is stronger at higher levels. More specifically, the relationship is almost twice as strong in countries with high press freedom than in countries with low press freedom ($b_{low} = 0.260, p < 0.001$; $b_{medium} = 0.369, p < 0.001$; $b_{high} = 0.477, p < 0.001$).

For misperceptions, we find a negative, significant interaction term ($p < 0.05$). As shown in the right plot of Figure 22, greater use of newspapers seems to be associated with reduced levels of misperceptions. In countries with high press freedom, while the coefficient is the largest, the effect is not significant due to a large standard error ($b = -1.65, p = 0.537$). This changes in countries with medium press freedom, where we find a negative association ($b = -0.105, p < 0.001$). In countries with low press freedom, there is no relationship ($b = -0.044, p = 0.868$).

Regarding education, again, we find no evidence of significant interactions between newspaper use and countries' education performance for either political knowledge ($p = 0.867$) or misperceptions ($p = 0.926$).

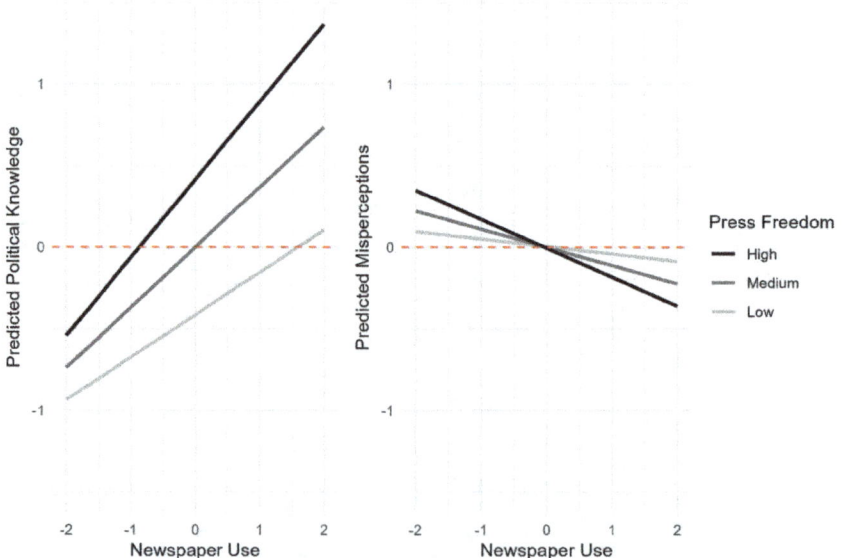

Figure 22 Interaction between newspaper use and press freedom on political knowledge (left plot) and misperceptions (right plot).

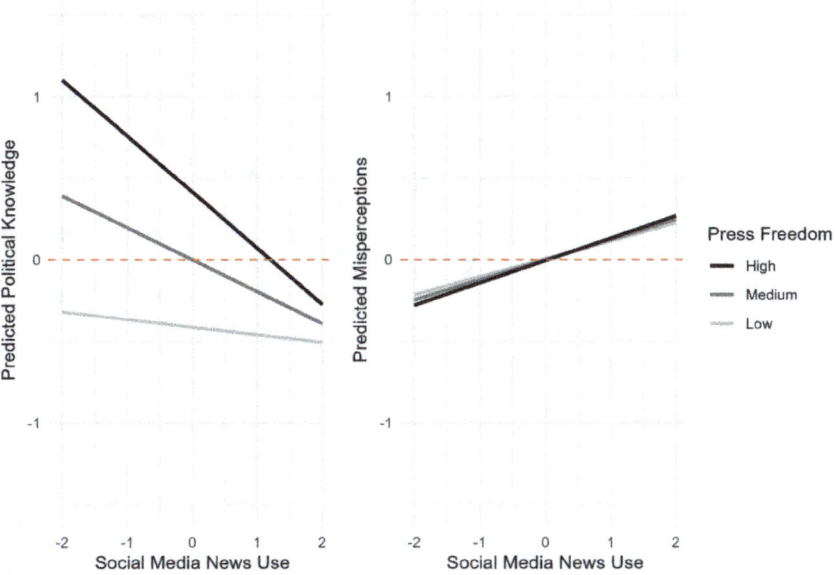

Figure 23 Interaction between social media use and press freedom on political knowledge (left plot) and misperceptions (right plot).

6.3.3 Media type – Social Media

Turning to the role of social media, we observe a statistically significant interaction between news use via social media and press freedom when predicting political knowledge ($p < 0.001$). As shown in Figure 23 (left plot), social media is associated with less political knowledge, especially in countries characterized by high levels of press freedom ($b = -0.344, p < 0.001$). This association is weaker at the average level of press freedom ($b = -0.196, p < 0.001$) and nonexistent in countries with lower levels of press freedom ($b = -0.047, p = 0.334$).

In contrast, we do not find any evidence that press freedom moderates the relationship between social media news use and misperceptions, as the interaction term is insignificant ($p = 0.498$). In other words, the positive main effect of social media news use on misperceptions ($p < 0.001$) remains about the same across different levels of press freedom (Figure 23, right plot).

Also, we find no evidence of a significant interaction between social media news use and countries' education performance for either political knowledge ($p = 0.22$) or misperceptions ($p = 0.195$).

6.3.4 Media Type – Messaging Services

Regarding the importance of using messaging services for news, the results show that greater reliance on messaging services for news is associated with

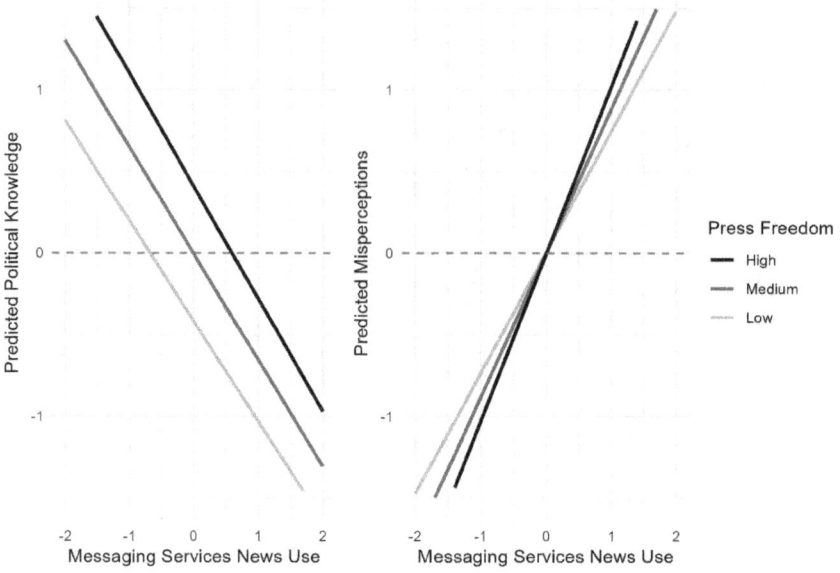

Figure 24 Interaction between messaging service use and press freedom on political knowledge (left plot) and misperceptions (right plot).

lower levels of political knowledge, regardless of different levels of press freedom, as the interaction term is insignificant ($p = 0.453$). Figure 24 (left plot) shows that the relationship is negative in all cases, just like the statistically significant main effect ($p < 0.001$).

We do, however, find a significant interaction between press freedom and the use of messaging services in the case of misperceptions ($p < 0.001$). As shown in Figure 24 (right plot), the association between consuming news via messaging services and the level of misperceptions is more pronounced in countries with higher levels of press freedom ($b_{low} = 0.740$, $p < 0.001$; $b_{medium} = 0.881$, $p < 0.001$; $b_{high} = 1.022$, $p < 0.001$). Even so, the general pattern remains the same, as greater news use via messaging services is associated with people holding more misperceptions across all contexts.

While we do not find evidence of a significant interaction between news consumption via messaging services and the countries' education levels in the case of misperceptions ($b = 0.203$; $p = 0.100$), there is a significant interaction when predicting political knowledge ($b = 0.465$; $p < 0.01$). While messenger services are negatively associated with political knowledge for all education levels, the relationship is stronger the lower the education performance of a country, as Figure 25 (left plot) shows ($b_{low} = -0.801$, $p < 0.001$; $b_{medium} = -0.689$, $p < 0.001$; $b_{high} = -0.576$, $p < 0.001$).

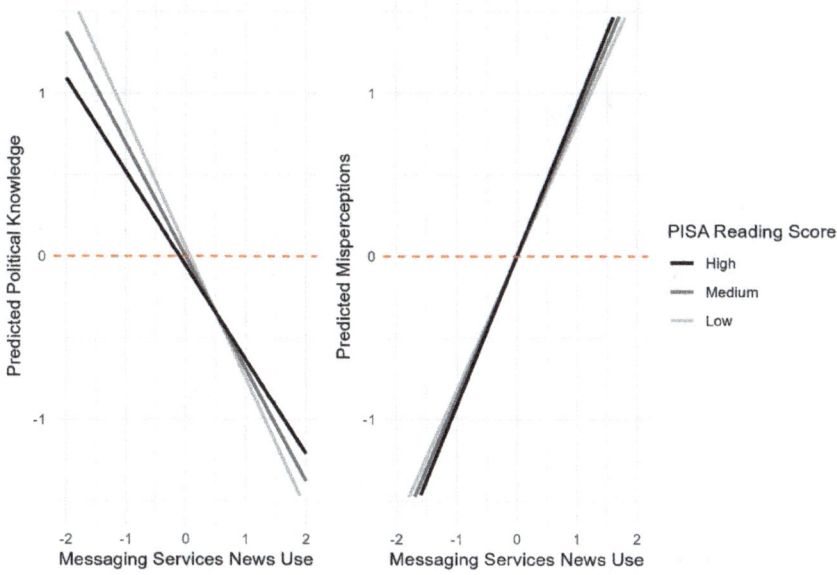

Figure 25 Interaction between messaging service use and countries' education performance on political knowledge (left plot) and misperceptions (right plot).

6.3.5 Mainstream News Media – Public Service versus Commercial Broadcasting

As noted earlier, not all broadcasters nor all newspapers are alike, and with respect to broadcasting, a key distinction is between public service and commercial broadcasters. The question is how this might influence the linkage with political knowledge and holding misperceptions, depending on the level of press freedom. To begin with political knowledge, the findings show that the positive relationship between consuming news from public service media and political knowledge is moderated by press freedom, as the interaction term is statistically significant ($p < 0.001$). In other words, while public service news consumption increases knowledge on average ($p < 0.001$), knowledge gains are larger the more the country is characterized by high press freedom ($b_{low} = 0.266$, $p < 0.001$; $b_{medium} = 0.666$, $p < 0.001$; $b_{high} = 1.066$, $p < 0.001$; see left plot of Figure 26).

As shown in previous sections, public service media contribute not only to greater political knowledge but also to decreased levels of misperceptions. Focusing on how this relationship varies across different levels of press freedom, we find that the interaction term is significant ($p < 0.01$). The contribution of public service broadcasting news to reduced misperceptions is stronger in countries with greater press freedom ($b_{low} = -0.373$, $p < 0.001$; $b_{medium} = -0.476$, $p < 0.001$; $b_{high} = -0.580$, $p < 0.001$; see right plot of Figure 26).

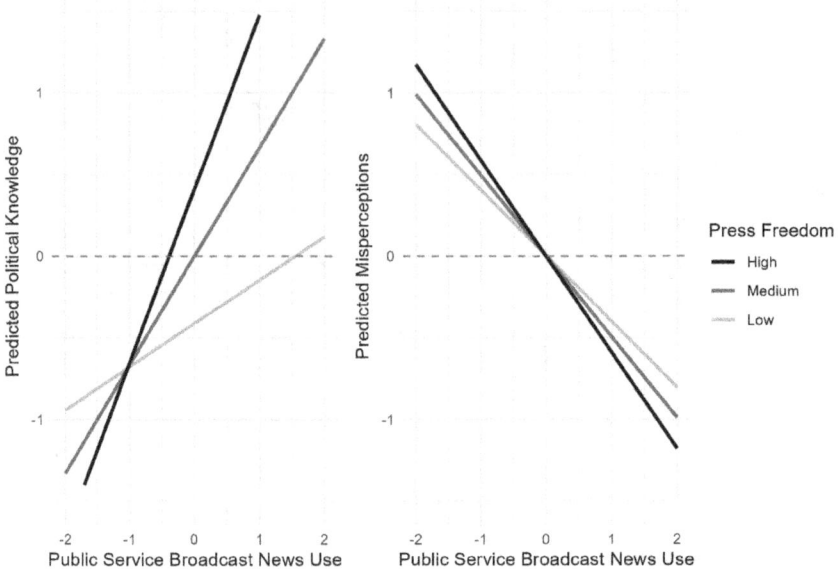

Figure 26 Interaction between public broadcasting use and press freedom on political knowledge (left plot) and misperceptions (right plot).

However, the overall impact of public service broadcasting on decreased misperceptions is robust in all countries.

As for education at the country level, we find a significant interaction between public broadcasting use and countries' education performance, both in the case of political knowledge ($b = 1.04$; $p < 0.001$) and misperceptions ($b = -0.576$; $p < 0.001$), as shown in Figure 27. In other words, the positive relationship between public service news consumption and political knowledge is stronger among countries with higher education levels ($b_{low} = 0.388$, $p < 0.001$; $b_{average} = 0.640$, $p < 0.001$; $b_{high} = 0.891$, $p < 0.001$). Similarly, the ability of public service news consumption to mitigate misperceptions is also more evident in countries with higher education levels ($b_{low} = -0.345$, $p < 0.001$; $b_{medium} = -0.485$, $p < 0.001$; $b_{high} = -0.625$, $p < 0.001$).

With respect to commercial broadcasting, we find that the interaction with press freedom when predicting political knowledge is statistically significant ($p < 0.05$). As Figure 28 (left plot) indicates, in countries with higher levels of press freedom, getting news from commercial broadcasting channels is more strongly associated with lower levels of political knowledge compared to countries with lower press freedom ($b_{low} = -0.324$, $p < 0.001$; $b_{medium} = -0.425$, $p < 0.001$; $b_{high} = -0.526$, $p < 0.001$). However, this negative relationship is observable in all countries, only to varying degrees.

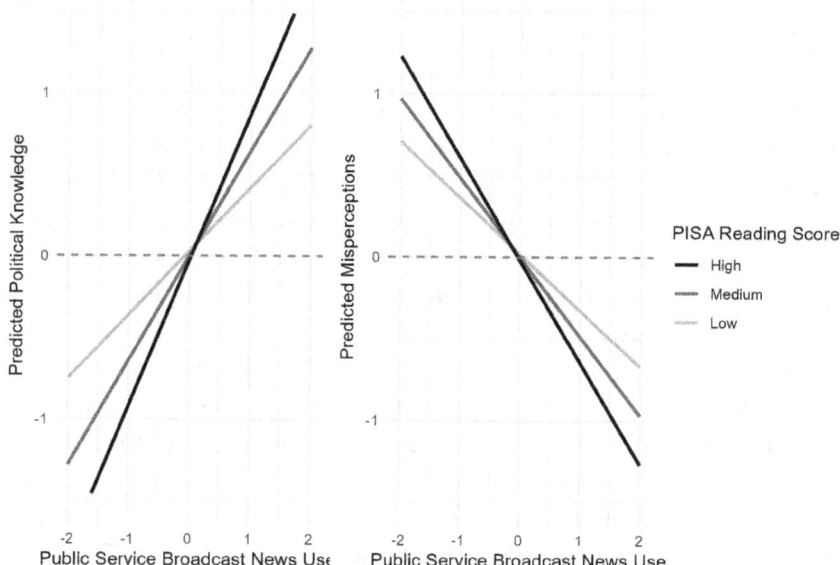

Figure 27 Interaction between public broadcasting use and countries' education performance on political knowledge (left plot) and misperceptions (right plot).

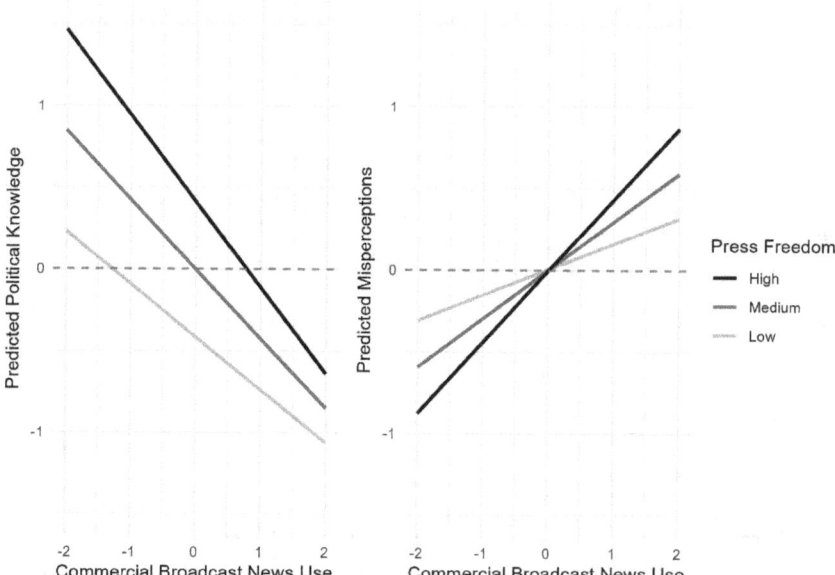

Figure 28 Interaction between commercial broadcasting use and press freedom on political knowledge (left plot) and misperceptions (right plot).

We also find that the contribution of commercial broadcasting news consumption to fostering misperceptions varies according to levels of press freedom (the interaction term is significant at $p < 0.001$). As Figure 28 (right plot) shows, in countries with higher levels of press freedom, higher levels of misperceptions are more strongly linked to news use via commercial broadcasters ($b_{low} = 0.157, p < 0.01$; $b_{medium} = 0.296, p < 0.001$; $b_{high} = 0.436, p < 0.001$). As before, while the associations vary according to different levels of press freedom, they are in the same direction across all contexts. In other words, the general pattern is that the use of commercial broadcasting is associated with more misperceptions.

Turning to education at the country level, we find a significant interaction with commercial broadcasting news consumption both when predicting political knowledge ($b = -0.578; p < 0.01$) and misperceptions ($b = 0.529; p < 0.01$), as visible in Figure 29. This indicates that, contrary to our initial expectations, the possible damaging implications of commercial broadcasting news consumption on reduced political knowledge and increased misperceptions are mostly evident in countries with higher education levels (Political Knowledge: $b_{low} = -0.178, p < 0.05$; $b_{average} = -0.318, p < 0.001$; $b_{high} = -0.458, p < 0.001$; Misperceptions: $b_{low} = 0.175, p < 0.01$; $b_{medium} = 0.303, p < 0.001$; $b_{high} = 0.432, p < 0.001$).

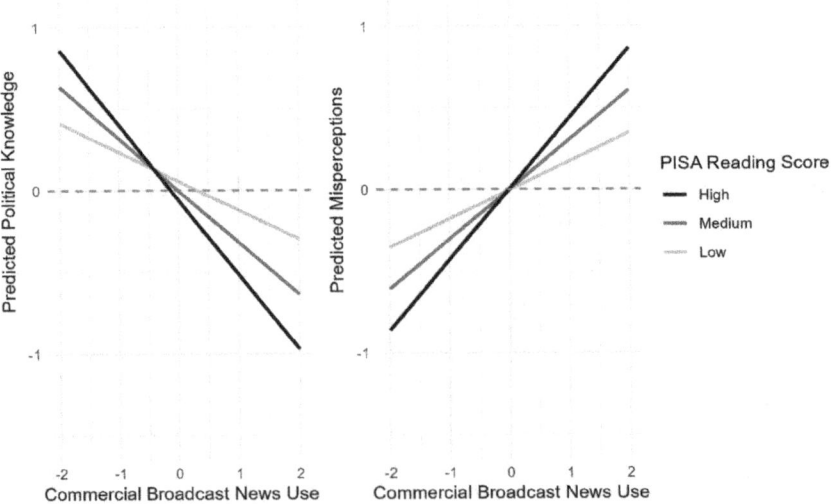

Figure 29 Interaction between commercial broadcasting use and countries' education performance on political knowledge (left plot) and misperceptions (right plot).

6.3.6 Mainstream News Media – Upmarket versus Mass-Market Newspapers

Focusing on upmarket newspapers, we find that the positive association between upmarket newspaper use and political knowledge varies with different levels of press freedom, as the interaction term is significant ($p < 0.001$). More specifically, Figure 30 (left plot) shows that upmarket newspapers have the strongest positive effect on political knowledge in countries with lower press freedom ($b = 0.920$, $p < 0.001$). The effect becomes weaker at average press freedom levels ($b = 0.629$, $p < 0.001$) and decreases to about one-third of its original strength in countries with higher levels of press freedom ($b = 0.337$, $p < 0.001$).

In contrast, the relationship between consuming upmarket newspapers and misperceptions is not moderated by press freedom, as the interaction term is statistically insignificant ($p = 0.211$; see the right plot of Figure 30).

The interaction between countries' education performance and upmarket newspaper use is not significant when predicting political knowledge ($p = 0.516$), but it is significant in the case of misperceptions ($b = 0.849$, $p < 0.001$). As shown in Figure 31 (right plot), upmarket newspaper use is positively associated with misperceptions in countries with higher education performance ($b = 0.284$, $p < 0.001$). This association does not exist in countries with average ($b = 0.078$, $p = 0.112$) and lower ($b = -0.128$, $p = 0.076$) education

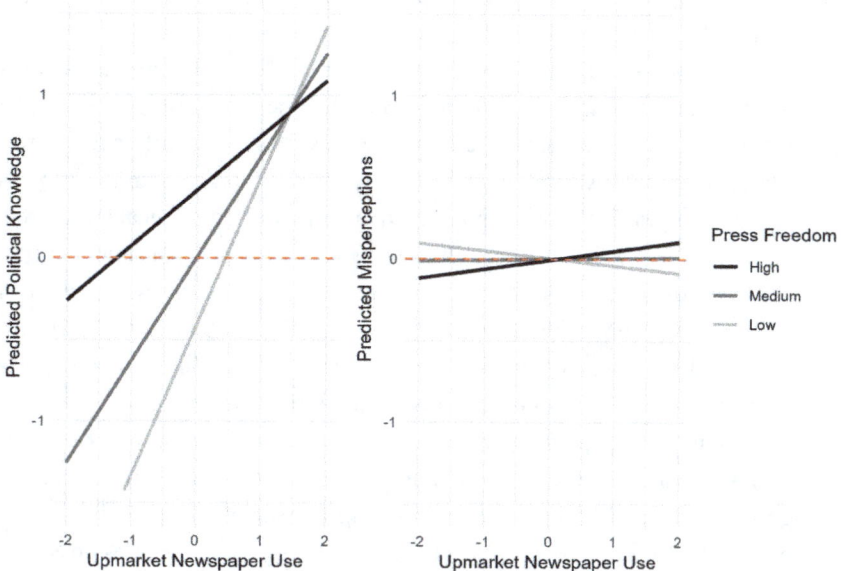

Figure 30 Interaction between upmarket newspaper use and press freedom on political knowledge (left plot) and misperceptions (right plot).

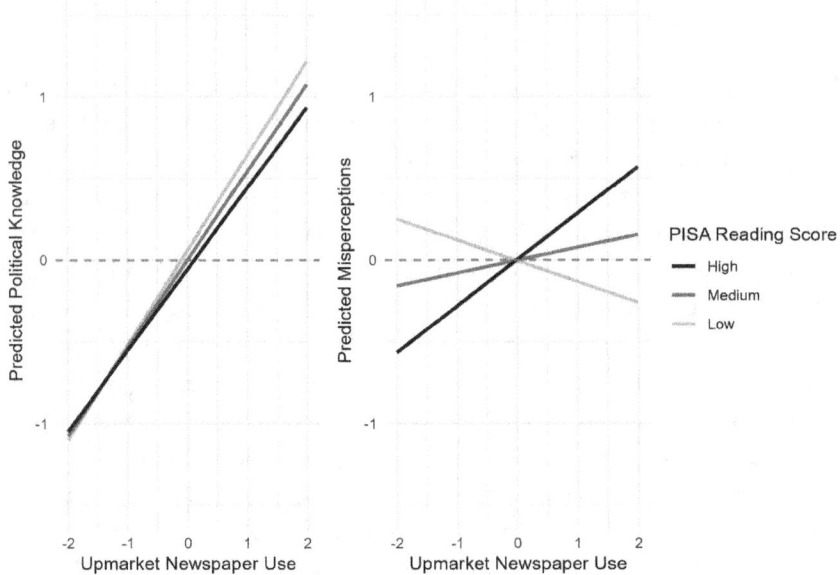

Figure 31 Interaction between upmarket newspaper use and countries' education performance on political knowledge (left plot) and misperceptions (right plot).

levels. These findings may help explain why the overall relationship between upmarket newspaper use and misperceptions was nonsignificant across the full sample (see Section 5).

Moving to mass-market newspaper use, the interaction with press freedom is statistically significant ($p < 0.001$), indicating that the relationship between the use of mass-market press and political knowledge varies across different levels of press freedom. As shown in Figure 32 (left plot), in countries with lower press freedom, the association between mass-market news use and political knowledge is negative ($b = -0.254, p < 0.001$). This relationship disappears in countries with average levels of press freedom ($b = -0.035, p = 0.385$) and reverses to positive in countries with high press freedom contexts ($b = 0.184, p < 0.001$). These results suggest that, depending on the media environment, the use of mass-market press products can, in fact, yield opposite effects on political knowledge.

In the context of misperceptions, we find a significant interaction effect ($p < 0.001$). As shown in Figure 32 (right plot), in countries with low press freedom, using mass-market newspapers is most strongly associated with holding misperceptions ($b = 0.467, p < 0.001$). This association weakens as press freedom increases, becoming about half as strong at average levels ($b = 0.226, p < 0.001$) and disappearing in high press freedom contexts ($b = -0.015, p = 0.749$).

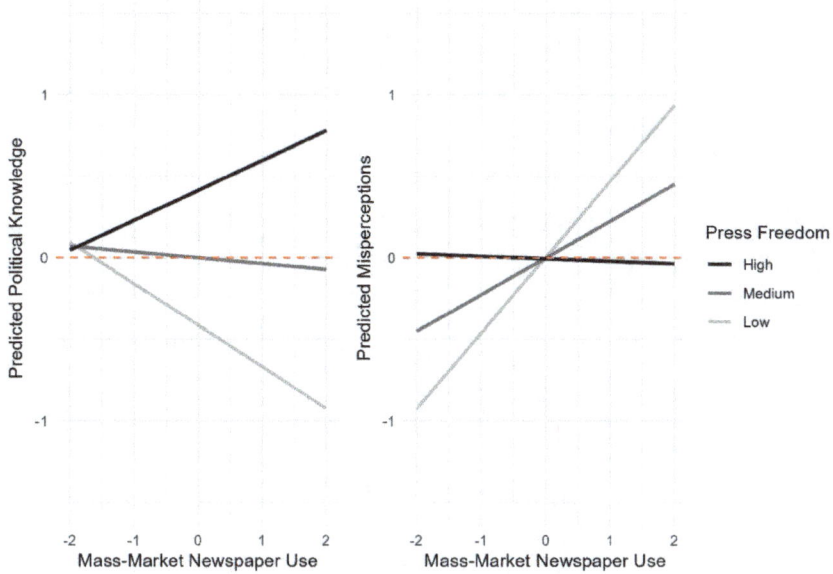

Figure 32 Interaction between mass-market newspaper use and press freedom on political knowledge (left plot) and misperceptions (right plot).

Finally, the interaction between consuming mass-market newspapers and countries' education performance is significant both for political knowledge ($b = 0.579$; $p < 0.01$) and misperceptions ($b = -0.913$; $p < 0.001$). As shown in Figure 33 (left plot), the positive relationship between mass-market news and political knowledge is especially evident in countries with high ($b = 0.296$, $p < 0.001$) and medium ($b = 0.156$, $p < 0.001$) levels of education performance. This association becomes insignificant in countries with lower education scores ($b = 0.015$, $p = 0.796$). In the case of misperceptions (right plot), consuming mass-market newspapers is associated with fewer misperceptions only in countries with high education scores ($b = -0.097$, $p < 0.05$), but this relationship is reversed and becomes positive in countries with medium ($b = 0.125$, $p < 0.001$) and, even more so, lower ($b = 0.346$, $p < 0.001$) education scores.

6.4 Conclusions

Summing up this section, in line with previous studies (Amsalem & Zoizner, 2023; Schäfer & Schemer, 2024; Shehata & Strömbäck, 2021; van Erkel & Van Aelst, 2021), we find that people generally gain more political knowledge from consuming traditional media compared to social media platforms. However, our comparative approach has allowed us to further extend this literature by highlighting the important role of macro-level factors in fostering

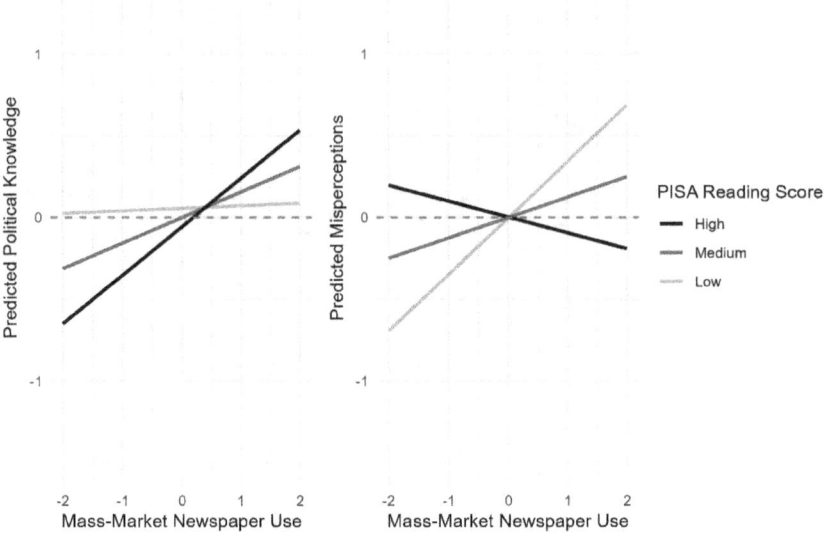

Figure 33 Interaction between mass-market newspaper use and countries' education performance on political knowledge (left plot) and misperceptions (right plot).

an informed citizenry. While we find that country-level education performance moderates the relationships between news use and knowledge, its impact is less consistent compared to the key role of press freedom in shaping these relationships.

Our results highlight the effectiveness of traditional media, and particularly public service broadcasters, in promoting political knowledge, with this relationship being amplified in certain contexts. First, it is especially evident in countries with a greater supply of high-quality political information, as indicated by higher levels of press freedom. In countries with greater press freedom, consuming news from traditional outlets, and in particular, watching news on public service broadcasters, is associated with more knowledge compared to countries with lower levels of press freedom. This underscores the importance of access to higher-quality, more informative content in freer media environments, which provide citizens with greater context, critical coverage of officials, and diverse perspectives in the news (Besley & Prat, 2006; Salgado et al., 2017).

One notable exception is when considering the relationship between upmarket press and political knowledge. People who consume upmarket newspapers are particularly well-informed in countries with lower (not higher) levels of press freedom. This suggests that upmarket newspapers may function as information and misinformation are produced and disseminated. Political information provided by traditional news media typically relies on professional journalistic practices such as verification, fact-checking, investigative reporting, and resource-intensive news production. Consequently, limitations on press freedom directly affect the quality of such information, which, in turn, shapes people's political knowledge. In contrast, misinformation can be created and spread rapidly by anyone online, without basically any effort at all and without any need for significant resources. This ease of production and dissemination allows misinformation to bypass traditional gatekeepers like journalists, making it less reliant on press freedom in a country.

The less consistent interactions in the context of misperceptions are also evident when considering countries' education performance as a macro-level moderator. While public service broadcasting is more effective in countries with higher education scores, the effects of consuming news from popular types of media sources are more mixed. For instance, commercial TV broadcasters tend to amplify misperceptions more in highly educated societies, whereas the effects of mass-market newspapers vary: they are generally more harmful in countries with lower education scores but can reduce misperceptions in more educated contexts.

This divergence may reflect differences in how different types of popular media sources present substantive political information alongside sensational or entertainment-driven content. Mass-market newspapers often contain a large volume of soft and low-quality news content, creating a sharper contrast with their more factual reporting (Brekken et al., 2013). In highly educated societies, audiences may be better equipped to identify and focus on the more substantive political content. In contrast, commercial TV tends to present a more even mix of emotional and factual content compared to mass-market newspapers (Brekken et al., 2013; Reinemann et al., 2017), making it harder to distinguish reliable information from lower-quality content that may contribute to misperceptions. These findings reinforce the conclusion that the availability and nature of political information are not the only factors shaping citizens' misperceptions. Citizens' cognitive abilities and skills in processing information and distinguishing between true and false claims also play a critical role.

6.5 Exploring Country Outliers: Deviations in the Relationship between News Use, Political Knowledge, and Misperceptions

So far, we have systematically examined the role of two macro-level factors in shaping the relationship between news use, political knowledge, and misperceptions. These analyses relied on pooled models that included all eighteen a unique and essential source of information in restricted media environments, enabling people to learn about social and political issues more effectively compared to other news sources (see also Stępińska et al., in press). In contrast, in freer media environments, the unique role of the upmarket press might be attenuated due to the more widespread availability of high-quality information across various news types and channels.

Second, the positive relationship between traditional media use and political knowledge is also stronger in contexts where citizens possess greater cognitive skills and experience in processing political information, as reflected in higher country-level education performance. For instance, we find that knowledge gains from public service broadcasters are most evident in countries with higher education scores. These findings suggest that the impact of traditional media on political knowledge depends not only on supply-side factors, such as the availability of high-quality information, but also on demand-side conditions. When the public has the skills needed to engage with and learn from political content, knowledge gains from traditional media are significantly enhanced.

We also find that the erosion of political knowledge, as a result of news consumption via newer media (social media platforms or messaging services) or commercial broadcasters, is especially evident in countries with high press freedom. In other words, the damaging effects of newer and more commercialized news sources on political knowledge are attenuated and smaller in more restricted media environments. Countries' educational performance generally does not moderate these relationships, except for messaging services, which are most detrimental to political knowledge in countries with lower education scores.

While macro-level factors, particularly press freedom, play a prominent role in shaping the relationship between news use and political knowledge, their moderating role in the context of misperceptions is more mixed. Focusing first on press freedom, our results show that newspapers and public service broadcasters are more effective at protecting people from misperceptions in countries with high press freedom. However, no similar patterns are observed for TV news use in general. The findings for newer media are also mixed: messaging services tend to lead to higher levels of misperceptions, particularly in high-press-freedom contexts, while the influence of using social media platforms does not vary with press freedom. Similarly, commercial TV broadcasters are more likely to amplify misperceptions in high-press-freedom environments, whereas mass-market newspapers are particularly damaging in restricted media environments with low press freedom.

The mixed findings regarding the role of press freedom in the context of misperceptions, compared to its relatively consistent role in shaping political knowledge, may arise from fundamental differences in how political countries in our sample. An alternative approach would be to analyze these relationships using media systems typologies, which cluster countries together based on features such as media markets, journalistic cultures, or media regulation. While such typologies offer valuable conceptual frameworks for comparative research, we are more cautious about directly relying on them for several reasons.

First, there is less agreement in the literature on how media systems should be categorized. While the classic Hallin and Mancini (2004) typology identifies three systems, subsequent studies propose a fourth system (Brüggemann et al., 2014) or a hybrid system that challenges earlier classifications (Humprecht et al., 2022). Other studies have proposed alternative typologies, particularly in relation to countries' resilience to online misinformation (Humprecht et al., 2020). These divergent typologies assign different countries to different systems, thus limiting the ability to apply a consistent classification across our sample.

Second, our empirical findings, presented in Sections 3–5, indicate that countries grouped together in existing media system typologies do not necessarily exhibit similar patterns in our data. For example, Poland and the US, or Austria and the UK, which are typically placed in different media systems, often behave in comparable ways and occasionally stand out as outliers in similar directions.

Given the conceptual variations and empirical discrepancies observed across countries, we are more cautious about applying crude media system categories as country-level explanations. Instead, we advocate for a more context-sensitive approach that can better reflect the patterns in our data. To examine cross-national deviations in the relationships between news use, political knowledge, and misperceptions, we adopt a country-specific approach, the results of which are presented in Sections 3–5, which analyze these relationships within each country individually. While country-specific analyses may have limited statistical power due to smaller sample sizes, they provide valuable insights into how news use, political knowledge, and misperceptions vary in specific case studies. As was shown earlier, our analyses found that three countries recurrently were outliers, namely Poland, Romania, and the US. While these countries are not extreme outliers in our sample (see Figure 20), they all exhibit associations between news use and both political knowledge and misperceptions that deviate substantially from the broader cross-national trends. The question is why. We propose several potential explanations for these deviations, addressing both theoretical and methodological considerations.

Among the most notable outliers in our sample are Poland and Romania. Starting with traditional media consumption, our findings reveal that in both countries, consuming newspapers and TV news has almost no impact on people's political knowledge levels, in contrast to the positive impact observed in most other countries (see Section 3). Moreover, in both Poland and Romania, we find some evidence (albeit not statistically significant at conventional levels) of a negative relationship between public service news use and political knowledge (see Section 5). This deviates from the generally positive role of public service broadcasting in fostering an informed citizenry across countries. Turning to newer media, we observe a minimal effect of messaging services on increased misperceptions in both of these countries (alongside Israel; see Section 4). In Romania, consuming news via social media is additionally positively associated with political knowledge, which contrasts with the overall negative relationship observed across the broader sample (see Section 3).

We believe these unique trends in Poland and Romania can be linked to their specific political and media conditions, as shown by their low rankings on the Press Freedom Index (see Figure 20). Both countries face significant government censorship of national media, ranking 38th (Romania) and 124th (Poland) globally in 2021, according to the V-Dem project (Coppedge et al., 2024). They are also characterized by weak democratic institutions compared to other countries in our sample. For instance, in the 2021 EIU Democracy Index, Romania ranked 61st and Poland 51st globally (Economist Intelligence Unit, 2022), while on V-Dem's Liberal Democracy Index for the same year, Romania ranked 55th and Poland 78th.

These low rankings reflect not only restrictions on high-quality journalistic content in Poland and Romania but also significant governmental influence over the flow of information, particularly in the news coverage provided by traditional news media and public service broadcasters (Štětka & Mihelj, 2024). Such conditions can undermine the ability of traditional news media, particularly public service broadcasters, to provide people with informative, diverse, and critical political coverage (Stępnik, 2023). This likely contributes to the lower ability of traditional news media to increase political knowledge. While recent studies suggest that political pressures may strengthen journalists' watchdog role in the Polish case (Stępińska et al., in press), our findings indicate that these efforts have limited success in increasing political knowledge, possibly due to declining media trust among the general public (Newman et al., 2023).

Conversely, these restrictive media environments may explain why newer media types hold fewer negative consequences in both countries and, in the Romanian case, even lead to positive knowledge gains from consuming news via social media. While traditional news media remain the central sources for information, social media have become an increasingly important news source in both countries (Buturoiu et al., 2023; Newman et al., 2023). People in more restricted media environments may particularly benefit from the advantages that alternative sources like social media offer when processing political news. For example, user discussions on social media can provide additional context and diverse perspectives that help people better process and understand political information—features that become especially valuable for knowledge gains when traditional news media are more restricted and less trustworthy (Besley & Prat, 2006; Salgado et al., 2017).

A second notable case is the US, which exhibits associations that differ from the overall trends observed across the cross-country sample. Political knowledge among American people in our study appears largely unaffected by news consumption across various media types. For instance, unlike other countries, there is no evidence of a positive relationship between political knowledge and news consumption via TV in general (Section 3) and public service broadcasters in particular (Section 5). Additionally, in the US context, using either social media or messaging services has a close-to-zero effect on political knowledge (Section 3). The only media sources in the US that demonstrate a positive association with people's political knowledge (albeit not statistically significant at conventional levels) are newspapers and commercialized broadcasters.

These findings may be partly explained by how political knowledge was measured in our study. The items used to assess political knowledge focused on topics related to both national and foreign affairs, such as the UN or NATO (see Section 2). However, many Americans tend to have limited knowledge of foreign affairs and are often inattentive to news on such issues (Baum & Potter, 2019). Political learning in this domain can therefore be expected to be minimal, with some exceptions. People may, for example, acquire some knowledge about politics indirectly as a by-product of seeking entertainment or by being exposed to soft news on traditional media outlets, which lowers the cognitive costs of engaging with such topics (Baum, 2002). This may help explain why commercial broadcasters in the US contribute modestly to people's knowledge of both national and foreign affairs.

Another notable result in the US context is that it is one of only two cases (alongside Poland) where newspaper use is associated with a relative increase in misperceptions (see Section 4). Given that TV news use in the US (as in the entire sample) is associated with lower levels of misperceptions, this finding is particularly striking. One explanation could be the rapid decline of local newspapers in the US, which has shifted Americans' media consumption habits toward national newspapers (Abernathy, 2018). National news media tend to focus more on national affairs, exposing readers to polarized elites (Darr et al., 2021) that often disrespect the truth and make more false statements on contested issues (Lasser et al., 2022; Mosleh & Rand, 2022). Alternatively, heightened competition among local newspapers might drive them to emphasize the polarizing rhetoric of national leaders, aligning their coverage with the partisan composition of their local communities (Bailard, 2023). In either case, whether Americans consume local or national newspapers, their reliance on partisan identities when interpreting political information in newspapers is likely to increase. This could contribute to greater misperceptions on contested issues such as COVID-19 or climate change. It should also be noted that the US media system is the most commercialized and competitive of the countries in our study, which may lead not only to lower news quality but also to increasing quality differences between different media depending on their audience composition (Baker, 2002; Hamilton, 2004; Usher, 2021).

7 Discussion

7.1 Main conclusions

This study started from the established idea that people learn about politics and relevant societal issues via the news media, an idea that can be put into question because of what we labeled the 'twin challenge of increased media choice'. The first challenge pertains to the growing number of people who, despite the abundance of news and other information, choose to avoid most news or only consume media that offer minimal hard news. This can leave people *uninformed* about what is happening in politics and society. Second, and more recently, there is a growing concern that people may form their beliefs based on false and misleading information, leading them to become *misinformed* about current political issues. This challenge has escalated alongside the success of newer digital media platforms that enable the rapid dissemination of content that does not adhere to traditional journalistic standards of verification, accuracy, and fact-checking.

We investigated both challenges based on data from a large survey in eighteen Western countries. Consistent with the existing literature, our results largely confirm the added value of staying informed through the use of traditional news media. Increased consumption of traditional news media, such as TV and newspapers, is generally associated with higher levels of knowledge. Delving deeper into the positive impact of traditional news media, we found that watching news programs from the public broadcaster, in particular, contributes to people's political knowledge. This is in line with several previous studies (Aalberg & Curran, 2012; Soroka et al., 2013; Strömbäck, 2017) and showcases that it remains valuable to invest public money in public service broadcasting, even in the digital era.

In contrast, consuming news from newer media sources, such as social media and messaging apps, is typically associated with lower knowledge about political matters. These 'newer' digital sources are also associated with people holding misperceptions on so-called contested issues, such as climate change or COVID-19. Here, traditional news media seem to limit belief in false statements, while 'newer' media rather strengthen those beliefs. Although social media platforms and messenger apps are often grouped together, their relationship with political knowledge is not identical. While using social media in most countries is not beneficial for learning about politics (see also Amsalem & Zoizner, 2023), the relationship between political knowledge and the use of messaging services is significantly negative. In other words, relying on messaging services for news is associated with less political knowledge.

How can these diverging findings be explained? First and foremost, content disseminated on messaging apps likely contains little news or other types of factual information. Even on a somewhat 'political' social media platform like Twitter/X, most people choose to follow celebrities rather than journalists or politicians (Wojcieszak et al., 2022). These low levels of consumption of news about politics or current affairs are probably even stronger on platforms like WhatsApp or Facebook Messenger, at least in the countries included in this study. In that sense, it is not surprising that messaging service apps keep people uninformed about politics. Even if people encounter political information on messaging services, it typically comes through peer-to-peer sharing, which often lacks contextual depth and editorial oversight. Such sharing tends to include simplified or incomplete interpretations of political events and may be characterized by reduced attention to details. These characteristics could help explain the relationship between news consumption via messaging services and lower levels of political knowledge.

Also, the correlation between the use of messaging services and people being misinformed is intriguing. Is it due to the lack of information to refute popular misbeliefs, or is misinformation actively spread through these channels, as some recent studies suggest (e.g., Kalogeropoulos & Rossini, 2023)? This question requires further research.

7.2 Do All People Benefit from Using the Media?

A classical issue in the study of the relationship between news media and political knowledge is the role of education. Research on the knowledge gap has often suggested that media use increases the existing differences in knowledge between lower- and higher-educated citizens. Our findings highlight that individual-level education indeed moderates the relationship between use of certain types of media and both political knowledge and misbeliefs. In particular, as we dive deeper into the added value of specific media channels, we find that while upmarket newspapers seem to reinforce existing knowledge advantages among the highly educated, public broadcasting and mass-market newspapers appear to offer more substantial gains for those with lower education. This suggests that more informative but also accessible news formats may help reduce knowledge gaps, whereas more demanding formats continue to privilege already advantaged groups. For misbeliefs, the relationship is more complex, as these more popular forms of media (mass-market newspapers and commercial TV) seem less beneficial for higher-educated citizens. Potentially, this might be due to existing political beliefs among these groups and the role of motivated reasoning. Future research should however dig deeper into this relationship. In general, our results show that lower-educated people benefit most from following TV news in acquiring knowledge on contested issues and limiting misbeliefs.

Interestingly, for newer media, educational-levels hardly ever played a moderating role. This seems to suggest that the rather negative effects of social media and messaging apps as tools for learning work across the board. Potentially, more variation can be found if studies distinguish between different platforms.

7.3 Different Countries, Same Findings?

The relationship between media use and political knowledge has received ample scholarly attention in recent decades but has rarely been studied among such a large number of countries. Since addressing country variation was a clear goal of this study, we conducted a more thorough exploration of whether and how knowledge measurements can be standardized across countries, a task that has only received limited attention in past studies. In terms of results, we focused on country variation in three main ways. First, by presenting the main findings on media use, knowledge, and misperceptions for each country individually (Sections 3–5). Second, by systematically analyzing the role of press freedom and countries' education performance as potential explanatory factors for the country variation we observed (Section 6). Third, by further exploring countries that deviate from the overall trends (Section 6.5).

What can we conclude from this comparative exercise? Overall, we find that variance at the country level is quite limited. In statistical terms, the reported ICCs for political knowledge (12 percent) and even more for misperceptions (3 percent) seem to suggest that differences in the relationship between media use and knowledge are better explained by individual factors than by country-level ones. More concretely, many of our findings are rather consistent across the eighteen countries under study. For instance, the negative relationship between using messaging services for news and political knowledge (and the opposite association with misperceptions) is consistently found across countries. Also, the positive relationship between watching public service broadcast news and political knowledge is remarkably stable across countries. Fourteen out of seventeen countries show a positive correlation, and for only three countries is there a negative but nonsignificant relationship. In contrast, watching the news on commercial broadcasting channels seems less beneficial for political knowledge, as this relationship is absent or negative in all but one country. For some types of media, there is more variation across countries. For instance, the correlation between political knowledge and using upmarket and mass-market media is less consistent across countries. In particular, the role of different types of newspapers in the context of misperceptions remains unclear and mixed across countries.

A potential explanation for these findings might be that some types of media are simply more comparable across countries than others. For instance, only a few highly popular messaging services are used worldwide, and they have almost identical features. This likely leads to similar usage patterns and findings in different contexts, although culture also matters. The same can be argued for the fairly consistent nonsignificant relationship between political knowledge and social media as a news source across countries. Some of the findings related to traditional news media probably can be linked to this argument. Despite varying regulations on public broadcasting corporations in Western democracies (Betzel & Ward, 2004; Cushion, 2012), they all tend to focus on hard news and current affairs reporting, and thereby on providing more opportunities to learn about politics and contested issues. The more diverging results we see with different types of newspapers may be due to the greater variation between types of newspapers across countries compared to the more straightforward distinction between public and commercial broadcasting. One of the key challenges when doing cross-national comparative research is always to identify what constitutes equivalent cases, and this is more challenging for newspapers than for broadcast news.

The fact that some patterns are relatively stable across countries does, however, not mean that there was no country variation. There was, and Section 6 clarifies that an important portion of the variation can be attributed to differences in press freedom and education levels across countries. Press freedom serves as a crucial indicator of the availability and quality of political information provided in any given country, while countries' education performance reflects citizens' capacity to make effective use of such information through skills such as reading comprehension or critical thinking. While we find that aggregate education levels only matter in some cases, our findings indicate that press freedom has a more consistent moderating role, particularly in shaping the relationship between news use and political knowledge. For example, higher levels of press freedom increase the effectiveness of traditional news media in raising political knowledge, and the damaging effects of newer media on political knowledge are attenuated in countries with less press freedom. In contrast, the moderating role of press freedom is less consistent in the context of misperceptions. We attribute this result to fundamental differences in how factual versus false information is produced and disseminated. Since misinformation can be easily created and spread by anyone online, it is less dependent on a country's press freedom levels, as it can readily bypass traditional journalistic gatekeepers.

Finally, one can rightfully argue that the relatively small country variations are due to the limited selection of countries. Including democracies in the Global South could have resulted in diverging findings (see for instance Altay et al., 2024). In that sense, it is no surprise that a country such as Poland 'behaves' differently in our study. This Eastern-European country was characterized by clear signs of democratic backsliding during the time of the study (Štětka & Mihelj, 2024). This challenged the "classical" insights on the role of traditional and newer outlets in shaping political knowledge and misperceptions. For instance, with the Polish public broadcaster becoming an agent of propaganda rather than of a reliable source of information, it became less of a place to learn about politics. This created stronger incentives for concerned people looking for trustworthy information to turn to alternative sources, including social media, compared to people in European countries less influenced by democratic erosion.

7.4 Limitations and Further Research

As with any study, our work and the generalizability of its findings are not without limitations. Moving beyond common issues that concern all survey research in the social sciences, we focus on four shortcomings related to news use and knowledge and suggest avenues for improvement in future research.

The most common challenge in this type of research is determining causality. Does news consumption increase knowledge, or is it rather that more knowledgeable people have a preference for more informative media? Since we rely on one cross-sectional survey, we are refraining from making clear causal claims and mainly speak about the relationship between media use and knowledge. Still, our theoretical framework and empirical analyses are based on the assumption that there is a learning effect from media use on political knowledge. This is in line with panel studies (e.g., Dimitrova et al., 2014; Ohme,

2020) and experiments (e.g., Allcott et al., 2020; Anspach et al., 2019) that have proven that frequent media use contributes to learning about politics. In reality, it is probably a reinforcing process, with higher-educated people following the news more and opting for more qualitative content, and in turn learning more from following these news outlets on a regular basis. We encourage future studies to further explore such longitudinal dynamics, particularly whether traditional news media, but also social and digital media, primarily serve to maintain knowledge gaps, gradually increase it among those with prior knowledge, or function as an equalizing force that helps people accumulate political knowledge regardless of their initial knowledge levels.

A second concern relates to measuring political knowledge across multiple countries. What do people know about politics, and what can or should we expect them to know? And how can this knowledge be operationalized and measured? The classical study by Delli Carpini and Keeter (1996) differentiated between knowledge on the rules of the game, the main actors, and the issues at stake. Since then, scholars have struggled to include multiple measures of different types of knowledge in their study (see also Barabas et al., 2014). These different conceptualizations and measurements of political knowledge pose several challenges for scholars, particularly when it comes to comparative studies. On the one hand, when focusing on media use, it makes little sense to focus only on the rules of the game or static political knowledge, as this strongly correlates with general levels of education. On the other hand, it is difficult to mainly focus on surveillance knowledge, that is, measuring knowledge of recent political events, as this type of knowledge is (mostly) highly different across countries. We therefore opted for questions that can be labeled as general political knowledge, but still related to global ongoing events like the pandemic and the war in Ukraine. Following the news is definitely helpful, but not always necessary to acquire this knowledge. This means that the correlation between media use and knowledge in this study potentially underestimates learning effects from using different types of media. Future research should, however, dig deeper into the longitudinal impact of media use and different types of political knowledge.

Third, our measurements of news use via social media and messaging services were based on a single item, which may result in a severe simplification of actual use. This ignores the varying amount of political information available on different platforms (e.g., X versus TikTok) as well as the multidimensional nature of social media use (Dvir-Gvirsman, 2022). For example, people may use social media platforms for reading news, posting about political events, or endorsing political actors or actions (Choi, 2016). Each of these behaviors might have a different impact on people's knowledge. Additionally, news use patterns matter significantly, as passive scrolling likely yields different learning outcomes than active engagement with news content (Nanz & Matthes, 2020). Hence, we encourage future research to further explore how different types of news use (e.g., passive versus active) across different platforms affect political knowledge and misperceptions.

Finally, to measure misperceptions, we relied on a rather new and innovative approach to ask participants in the survey about so-called contested issues (Damstra et al., 2023; Vliegenthart et al., 2023). To overcome influence from the national contexts, we were limited to "global" issues such as climate change and COVID-19, which are not confined by national borders. The challenge here was that some of these statements were not considered as difficult or discriminating in each country, which meant that we ended up using only four out of eight items to form a cohesive scale to compare misperceptions across countries (see Section 2). Thus, a key challenge for future research on the impact of media use on misperceptions is to identify ways of measuring misperceptions that allow for cross-national comparative research. An additional challenge is to investigate misperceptions on issues that are independent of ideological beliefs. The topics of COVID-19 vaccines and climate change that were used in this study are more widely doubted and instrumentalized on the political right, making right-wing citizens seem more prone to holding misperceptions. Future research should include issues that are also more controversial across the political spectrum in order to generalize findings.

In the present study, we also treat misperceptions as a continuous variable ranging from high knowledge to misperceptions, with "Don't know" responses falling in between. As shown by Lindgren et al. (2022), it is, however, a challenge to separate the informed (who answer correctly), the uninformed (who indicate uncertainty), and the misinformed (who answer incorrectly). In theory, the distinction is quite clear-cut. Empirically, it is much more complicated, among other things because people might guess, be more or less willing to guess when they do not know, and withhold their true response. Addressing the conceptual-operational gap between (lack of) knowledge and (mis)perceptions is, hence, an important task for future research. It is also as important for comparative research to secure equivalence across countries in the measurement of misperceptions as it is with knowledge. In other words, scholars need to devote more time and effort to pretesting knowledge items that are equivalent across countries and vary enough in difficulty.

These limitations notwithstanding, this is one of the most comprehensive and in-depth cross-national analyses of the relationship between the use of different types of media, political knowledge, and misperceptions hitherto. Although there are many nuances, it has shown that traditional news media, despite all media environmental changes over the last decade, still matters and still are able to help inform people, including those with lower levels of education who can be considered more vulnerable to remaining uninformed or becoming misinformed. This holds particularly true for public service broadcasting. Traditional news media may also help counteract misperceptions. It has also shown that using newer digital media, such as social media platforms and messaging services, is typically negatively related to political knowledge and positively related to misperceptions. And it has shown that press freedom is important not only in itself but also for explaining country variation and why the effects of using certain media types differ across countries.

From a democratic perspective, these findings are important. Moving forward, the challenge that many people are uninformed or misinformed rather than informed will probably not descend. The same holds for the trend that many decrease their use of traditional news media, instead relying on social media platforms, messaging services, and political alternative media. Based on our findings, there are, hence, strong reasons to develop policies that might shield traditional news media from both political and economic pressures where they are strong, strengthen them where they are weaker, and encourage greater use of them.

References

Aalberg, T., & Curran, J. (Eds.). (2012). *How media inform democracy: A comparative approach*. Routledge.

Aalberg, T., & Cushion, S. (2016). *Public service broadcasting, hard news, and citizens' knowledge of current affairs* (Vol. 1). Oxford University Press. https://doi.org/10.1093/acrefore/9780190228637.013.38.

Aarts, K., & Semetko, H. A. (2003). The Divided Electorate: Media Use and Political Involvement. *The Journal of Politics*, *65*(3), 759–784. https://doi.org/10.1111/1468-2508.00211.

Abernathy, P. M. (2018). *The expanding news desert*. Center for Innovation and Sustainability in Local Media, School of Media and . . . . www.cislm.org/wp-content/uploads/2018/10/The-Expanding-News-Desert-10_14-Web.pdf.

Albrecht, M. M. (2023). *Trumping the media: Politics and democracy in the post-truth era*. Bloomsbury Academic.

Allcott, H., Braghieri, L., Eichmeyer, S., & Gentzkow, M. (2020). The Welfare Effects of Social Media. *American Economic Review*, *110*(3), 629–676.

Allcott, H., & Gentzkow, M. (2017). Social Media and Fake News in the 2016 Election. *Journal of Economic Perspectives*, *31*(2), 211–236. https://doi.org/10.1257/jep.31.2.211.

Allcott, H., Gentzkow, M., & Yu, C. (2019). Trends in the Diffusion of Misinformation on Social Media. *Research & Politics*, *6*(2), 1–8.

Altay, S., Nielsen, R. K., & Fletcher, R. (2024). News Can Help! The Impact of News Media and Digital Platforms on Awareness of and Belief in Misinformation. *The International Journal of Press/Politics*, *29*(2), 459–484. https://doi.org/10.1177/19401612221148981.

Amsalem, E., & Zoizner, A. (2023). Do People Learn about Politics on Social Media? A Meta-Analysis of 76 Studies. *Journal of Communication*, *73*(1), 3–13. https://doi.org/10.1093/joc/jqac034.

Andersen, K., Ohme, J., Bjarnøe, C., et al. (2021). *Generational gaps in political media use and civic engagement: From baby boomers to generation Z*. Routledge.

Andersen, K., Shehata, A., Skovsgaard, M., & Strömbäck, J. (2024). Selective News Avoidance: Consistency and Temporality. *Communication Research*. https://doi.org/10.1177/00936502231221689.

Andersen, K., & Strömbäck, J. (2021). Media Platforms and Political Learning: The Democratic Challenge of News Consumption on Computers and Mobile Devices. *International Journal of Communication*, *15*, 20.

Anspach, N. M., Jennings, J. T., & Arceneaux, K. (2019). A Little Bit of Knowledge: Facebook's News Feed and Self-perceptions of Knowledge. *Research & Politics*, *6*(1). https://doi.org/10.1177/2053168018816189.

Arechar, A. A., Allen, J., Berinsky, A. J., et al. (2023). Understanding and Combatting Misinformation across 16 Countries on Six Continents. *Nature Human Behaviour*, *7*(9), 1502–1513.

Aslett, K., Sanderson, Z., Godel, W., et al. (2024). Online Searches to Evaluate Misinformation Can Increase Its Perceived Veracity. *Nature*, *625*(7995), 548–556.

Bail, C. (2021). *Breaking the social media prism: How to make our platforms less polarizing*. Princeton University Press.

Bailard, C. S. (2023). Do Local Newspapers Mitigate the Effects of the Polarized National Rhetoric on COVID-19? *The International Journal of Press/Politics*, *28*(4), 929–951. https://doi.org/10.1177/19401612211072774.

Baker, C. E. (2002). *Media, markets, and democracy*. Cambridge University Press.

Bakshy, E., Messing, S., & Adamic, L. A. (2015). Exposure to Ideologically Diverse News and Opinion on Facebook. *Science*, *348*(6239), 1130–1132. https://doi.org/10.1126/science.aaa1160.

Barabas, J., Jerit, J., Pollock, W., & Rainey, C. (2014). The Question(s) of Political Knowledge. *American Political Science Review*, *108*(4), 840–855. https://doi.org/10.1017/S0003055414000392.

Baum, M. A. (2002). Sex, Lies and War: How Soft News Brings Foreign Policy to the Inattentive Public. *The American Political Science Review*, *96*(1), 91–109.

Baum, M. A. (2003). Soft News and Political Knowledge: Evidence of Absence or Absence of Evidence? *Political Communication*, *20*(2), 173–190. https://doi.org/10.1080/10584600390211181.

Baum, M. A., & Potter, P. B. K. (2019). Media, Public Opinion, and Foreign Policy in the Age of Social Media. *The Journal of Politics*, *81*(2), 747–756. https://doi.org/10.1086/702233.

Beckers, K., Van Aelst, P., Verhoest, P., & d'Haenens, L. (2021). What Do People Learn from Following the News? A Diary Study on the Influence of Media Use on Knowledge of Current News Stories. *European Journal of Communication*, *36*(3), 254–269. https://doi.org/10.1177/0267323120978724.

Benkler, Y., Faris, R., & Roberts, H. (2018). *Network propaganda: Manipulation, disinformation, and radicalization in American politics*. Oxford University Press.

Bennett, W. L., Lawrence, R. G., & Livingston, S. (2007). *When the press fails: Political power and the news media from Iraq to Katrina*. University of Chicago Press.

Bergmann, E. (2025). *Weaponizing conspiracy theories*. Routledge.

Bergström, A., Strömbäck, J., & Arkhede, S. (2019). Towards Rising Inequalities in Newspaper and Television News Consumption? A Longitudinal Analysis, 2000–2016. *European Journal of Communication*, *34*(2), 175–189. https://doi.org/10.1177/0267323119830048.

Berlinski, N., Doyle, M., Guess, A. M., et al. (2023). The Effects of Unsubstantiated Claims of Voter Fraud on Confidence in Elections. *Journal of Experimental Political Science*, *10*(1), 34–49. https://doi.org/10.1017/XPS.2021.18.

Besley, T., & Prat, A. (2006). Handcuffs for the Grabbing Hand? Media Capture and Government Accountability. *American Economic Review*, *96*(3), 720–736.

Betzel, M., & Ward, D. (2004). The Regulation of Public Service Broadcasters in Western Europe. *Trends in Communication*, *12*(1), 47–62. https://doi.org/10.1207/s15427439tc1201_5.

Blekesaune, A., Elvestad, E., & Aalberg, T. (2012). Tuning out the World of News and Current Affairs – An Empirical Study of Europe's Disconnected Citizens. *European Sociological Review*, *28*(1), 110–126. https://doi.org/10.1093/esr/jcq051.

Bode, L. (2016). Political News in the News Feed: Learning Politics from Social Media. *Mass Communication and Society*, *19*(1), 24–48. https://doi.org/10.1080/15205436.2015.1045149.

Bollen, K. A. (1989). *Structural equations with latent variables* (Vol. 210). John Wiley & Sons.

Bos, L., Kruikemeier, S., & de Vreese, C. (2016). Nation Binding: How Public Service Broadcasting Mitigates Political Selective Exposure. *PLOS ONE*, *11*(5), e0155112. https://doi.org/10.1371/journal.pone.0155112.

Boukes, M. (2019). Social Network Sites and Acquiring Current Affairs Knowledge: The Impact of Twitter and Facebook Usage on Learning about the News. *Journal of Information Technology & Politics*, *16*(1), 36–51. https://doi.org/10.1080/19331681.2019.1572568.

Brekken, T., Thorbjørnsrud, K., & Aalberg, T. (2013). News Substance: The Relative Importance of Soft and De-contextualized news. In T. Aalberg & J. Curran (Eds.), *How media inform democracy: A comparative approach* (pp. 64–78). Routledge.

Broda, E., & Strömbäck, J. (2024). Misinformation, Disinformation, and Fake News: Lessons from an Interdisciplinary, Systematic Literature Review. *Annals of the International Communication Association*, *48*(2), 139–166. https://doi.org/10.1080/23808985.2024.2323736.

Brüggemann, M., Engesser, S., Büchel, F., Humprecht, E., & Castro, L. (2014). Hallin and Mancini Revisited: Four Empirical Types of Western Media Systems: Hallin and Mancini Revisited. *Journal of Communication*, *64*(6), 1037–1065. https://doi.org/10.1111/jcom.12127.

Bruns, A. (2018). *Gatewatching and news curation*. Peter Lang US. https://doi.org/10.3726/b13293.

Bruns, A., Harrington, S., & Hurcombe, E. (2020). "Corona? 5G? or Both?": The Dynamics of COVID-19/5G Conspiracy Theories on Facebook. *Media International Australia*, *177*(1), 12–29. https://doi.org/10.1177/1329878X20946113.

Butter, M. (2020). *The nature of conspiracy theories*. Polity.

Buturoiu, R., Corbu, N., & Boțan, M. (2023). *Patterns of news consumption in a high-choice media environment: A Romanian perspective*. Springer Nature Switzerland. https://doi.org/10.1007/978-3-031-41954-6.

Carey, J. M., Guess, A. M., Loewen, P. J., et al. (2022). The Ephemeral Effects of Fact-Checks on COVID-19 Misperceptions in the United States, Great Britain and Canada. *Nature Human Behaviour*, *6*(2), 236–243.

Carlson, M., Robinson, S., & Lewis, S. C. (2021). *News after Trump: Journalism's crisis of relevance in a changed media culture*. Oxford University Press.

Castro, L., Strömbäck, J., Esser, F., et al. (2022). Navigating High-Choice European Political Information Environments: A Comparative Analysis of News User Profiles and Political Knowledge. *The International Journal of Press/Politics*, *27*(4), 827–859. https://doi.org/10.1177/19401612211012572.

Castro-Herrero, L., Nir, L., & Skovsgaard, M. (2018). Bridging Gaps in Cross-Cutting Media Exposure: The Role of Public Service Broadcasting. *Political Communication*, *35*(4), 542–565. https://doi.org/10.1080/10584609.2018.1476424.

Chadwick, A. (2013). *The hybrid media system: Politics and power*. Oxford University Press.

Chadwick, A., Vaccari, C., & Kaiser, J. (2022). The Amplification of Exaggerated and False News on Social Media: The Roles of Platform Use, Motivations, Affect, and Ideology. *American Behavioral Scientist*, *69*(2), 113–130. https://doi.org/10.1177/00027642221118264.

Chaffee, S. H., & Kanihan, S. F. (1997). Learning about Politics from the Mass Media. *Political Communication*, *14*, 421–430.

Chalmers, R. P. (2012). Mirt: A Multidimensional Item Response Theory Package for the R Environment. *Journal of Statistical Software*, *48*, 1–29.

Choi, J. (2016). Why Do People Use News Differently on SNSs? An Investigation of the Role of Motivations, Media Repertoires, and

Technology Cluster on Citizens' News-Related Activities. *Computers in Human Behavior*, *54*, 249–256.
Cook, T. E. (2005). *Governing with the news: The news media as a political institution* (2nd ed., Vol. 2005). University of Chicago Press.
Coppedge, M., Gerring, J., Knutsen, C. H., et al. (2024). *V-Dem Dataset v14* (Version 14) [Dataset]. University of Gothenburg. https://doi.org/10.23696/MCWT-FR58.
Cushion, S. (2012). *The democratic value of news: Why public service media matter*. Palgrave Macmillan.
Cushion, S. (2024). *Beyond mainstream media: Alternative media and the future of journalism*. Routledge.
Dahl, R. A. (1998). *On democracy*. Princeton University Press.
Damstra, A., Vliegenthart, R., Boomgaarden, H., et al. (2023). Knowledge and the News: An Investigation of the Relation between News Use, News Avoidance, and the Presence of (Mis)beliefs. *The International Journal of Press/Politics*, *28*(1), 29–48. https://doi.org/10.1177/19401612211031457.
Darr, J. P., Hitt, M. P., & Dunaway, J. L. (2021). *Home style opinion: How local newspapers can slow polarization* (1st ed.). Cambridge University Press. https://doi.org/10.1017/9781108950930.
De Vreese, C. H., & Boomgaarden, H. (2006). News, Political Knowledge and Participation: The Differential Effects of News Media Exposure on Political Knowledge and Participation. *Acta Politica*, *41*, 317–341. https://doi.org/10.1057/palgrave.ap.5500164.
De Vreese, C. H., Esser, F., & Hopmann, D. N. (2017). *Comparing political journalism*. Routledge.
de Zúñiga, H. G., Marné, H. M., Goyanes, M., & Scheffauer, R. (2024). *Social media democracy mirage: How social media news fuels a politically uninformed participatory democracy* (1st ed.). Cambridge University Press. https://doi.org/10.1017/9781009053266.
Delli Carpini, M. X., & Keeter, S. (1993). Measuring Political Knowledge: Putting First Things First. *American Journal of Political Science*, *37*(4), 1179–1206.
Delli Carpini, M. X., & Keeter, S. (1996). *What Americans know about politics and why it matters*. Yale University Press.
Dimitrova, D. V., Shehata, A., Strömbäck, J., & Nord, L. W. (2014). The Effects of Digital Media on Political Knowledge and Participation in Election Campaigns: Evidence from Panel Data. *Communication Research*, *41*(1), 95–118. https://doi.org/10.1177/0093650211426004.
Drew, D., & Weaver, D. (2006). Voter Learning in the 2004 Presidential Election: Did the Media Matter? *Journalism & Mass Communication Quarterly*, *83*(1), 25–42.

Dvir-Gvirsman, S. (2022). Understanding News Engagement on Social Media: A Media Repertoire Approach. *New Media & Society*, *24*(8), 1791–1812.

Economist Intelligence Unit. (2022). *Democracy Index 2021.* www.eiu.com/public/topical_report.aspx?campaignid=DemoIndex21.

Edgerly, S., Thorson, K., & Wells, C. (2018). Young Citizens, Social Media, and the Dynamics of Political Learning in the U.S. Presidential Primary Election. *American Behavioral Scientist*, *62*(8), 1042–1060. https://doi.org/10.1177/0002764218764236.

Eggers, A. C., Garro, H., & Grimmer, J. (2021). No Evidence for Systematic Voter Fraud: A Guide to Statistical Claims about the 2020 Election. *Proceedings of the National Academy of Sciences*, *118*(45), e2103619118. https://doi.org/10.1073/pnas.2103619118.

Elo, K., & Rapeli, L. (2010). Determinants of Political Knowledge: The Effects of the Media on Knowledge and Information. *Journal of Elections, Public Opinion and Parties*, *20*(1), 133–146. https://doi.org/10.1080/17457280903450799.

Elvestad, E., & Phillips, A. (2018). *Misunderstanding news audiences: Seven myths of the social media era*. Routledge.

Enders, A. M., Uscinski, J. E., Klofstad, C. A., et al. (2021). The 2020 Presidential Election and Beliefs about Fraud: Continuity or Change? *Electoral Studies*, *72*, 102366. https://doi.org/10.1016/j.electstud.2021.102366.

Espeland, E. (2024). The Dynamics of Political Interest and News Media Avoidance: A Generational and Longitudinal Perspective. *Journalism Studies*, *25*(12), 1–22. https://doi.org/10.1080/1461670X.2024.2366338.

Esser, F., de Vreese, C. H., Strömbäck, J., et al. (2012). Political Information Opportunities in Europe: A Longitudinal and Comparative Study of Thirteen Television Systems. *The International Journal of Press/Politics*, *17*(3), 247–274. https://doi.org/10.1177/1940161212442956.

Esser, F., & Hanitzsch, T. (Eds.). (2012). *Handbook of comparative communication research*. Routledge. https://doi.org/10.4324/9780203149102.

Eveland, W. P. (2001). The Cognitive Mediation Model of Learning From the News: Evidence from Nonelection, Off-Year Election, and Presidential Election Contexts. *Communication Research*, *28*(5), 571–601. https://doi.org/10.1177/009365001028005001.

Eveland, W. P., & Scheufele, D. A. (2000). Connecting News Media Use with Gaps in Knowledge and Participation. *Political Communication*, *17*(3), 215–237. https://doi.org/10.1080/105846000414250.

Flaxman, S., Goel, S., & Rao, J. M. (2016). Filter Bubbles, Echo Chambers, and Online News Consumption. *Public Opinion Quarterly*, *80*(S1), 298–320. https://doi.org/10.1093/poq/nfw006.

Fletcher, R., Robertson, C. T., & Nielsen, R. K. (2021). How Many People Live in Politically Partisan Online News Echo Chambers in Different Countries? *Journal of Quantitative Description: Digital Media, 1*, 1–56. https://doi.org/10.51685/jqd.2021.020.

Flynn, D. J., Nyhan, B., & Reifler, J. (2017). The Nature and Origins of Misperceptions: Understanding False and Unsupported Beliefs about Politics: Nature and Origins of Misperceptions. *Political Psychology, 38*, 127–150. https://doi.org/10.1111/pops.12394.

Fotakis, E. A., & Simou, E. (2023). Belief in COVID-19 Related Conspiracy Theories around the Globe: A Systematic Review. *Health Policy, 137*, 104903. https://doi.org/10.1016/j.healthpol.2023.104903.

Fraile, M., & Iyengar, S. (2014). Not All News Sources Are Equally Informative: A Cross-National Analysis of Political Knowledge in Europe. *The International Journal of Press/Politics, 19*(3), 275–294. https://doi.org/10.1177/1940161214528993.

Garrett, R. K., & Bond, R. M. (2021). Conservatives' Susceptibility to Political Misperceptions. *Science Advances, 7*(23), eabf1234. https://doi.org/10.1126/sciadv.abf1234.

Garrett, R. K., & Stroud, N. J. (2014). Partisan Paths to Exposure Diversity: Differences in Pro- and Counterattitudinal News Consumption. *Journal of Communication, 64*(4), 680–701. https://doi.org/10.1111/jcom.12105.

Garrett, R. K., Weeks, B. E., & Neo, R. L. (2016). Driving a Wedge between Evidence and Beliefs: How Online Ideological News Exposure Promotes Political Misperceptions: Driving a Wedge between Evidence and Beliefs. *Journal of Computer-Mediated Communication, 21*(5), 331–348. https://doi.org/10.1111/jcc4.12164.

Gehle, L., Hameleers, M., Tulin, M., et al. (2024). Misinformation Detection in the Context of the Russian Invasion of Ukraine: Evidence from Original Survey Data Collected in 19 Democracies. *International Journal of Public Opinion Research, 36*(3), edad040. https://doi.org/10.1093/ijpor/edad040.

Gil De Zúñiga, H., & Goyanes, M. (2023). Fueling Civil Disobedience in Democracy: WhatsApp News Use, Political Knowledge, and Illegal Political Protest. *New Media & Society, 25*(12), 3500–3520. https://doi.org/10.1177/14614448211047850.

Gil de Zúñiga, H., Jung, N., & Valenzuela, S. (2012). Social Media Use for News and Individuals' Social Capital, Civic Engagement and Political Participation. *Journal of Computer-Mediated Communication, 17*(3), 319–336. https://doi.org/10.1111/j.1083-6101.2012.01574.x.

Glüer, K., & Wikforss, Å. (2022). What Is Knowledge Resistance? In J. Strömbäck, A. Wikforss, K. Glüer, T. Lindholm, & H. Oscarsson (Eds.),

Knowledge resistance in high-choice information environments (pp. 29–48). Routledge.

Graber, D. (1990). Seeing Is Remembering: How Visuals Contribute to Learning from Television News. *Journal of Communication, 40*, 134–155.

Grinberg, N., Joseph, K., Friedland, L., Swire-Thompson, B., & Lazer, D. (2019). Fake News on Twitter during the 2016 U.S. Presidential Election. *Science, 363*(6425), 374–378. https://doi.org/10.1126/science.aau2706.

Grönlund, K., & Milner, H. (2006). The Determinants of Political Knowledge in Comparative Perspective. *Scandinavian Political Studies, 29*(4), 386–406. https://doi.org/10.1111/j.1467-9477.2006.00157.x.

Guess, A. M. (2021). (Almost) Everything in Moderation: New Evidence on Americans' Online Media Diets. *American Journal of Political Science, 65*(4), 1007–1022. https://doi.org/10.1111/ajps.12589.

Hallin, D. C., & Mancini, P. (2004). *Comparing media systems: Three models of media and politics*. Cambridge University Press.

Hameleers, M. (2021). *Populist disinformation in fragmented information settings: Understanding the nature and persuasiveness of populist and post-factual communication*. Routledge.

Hamilton, J. T. (2004). *All the news that's fit to sell. How the market transforms information into news*. Princeton University Press.

Hanitzsch, T., Hanusch, F., Mellado, C., et al. (2011). Mapping Journalism Cultures across Nations: A Comparative Study of 18 Countries. *Journalism Studies, 12*(3), 273–293. https://doi.org/10.1080/1461670X.2010.512502.

Hart, W., Albarracín, D., Eagly, A. H., et al. (2009). Feeling Validated versus Being Correct: A Meta-Analysis of Selective Exposure to Information. *Psychological Bulletin, 135*(4), 555–588. https://doi.org/10.1037/a0015701.

Haugsgjerd, A., Hesstvedt, S., & Karlsen, R. (2021). Increased Media Choice and Political Knowledge Gaps: A Comparative Longitudinal Study of 18 Established Democracies 1995–2015. *Political Communication, 38*(6), 731–750. https://doi.org/10.1080/10584609.2020.1868633.

Hindman, M. (2009). *The myth of digital democracy*. Princeton University Press.

Hochschild, J. L., & Einstein, L. (2015). *Do facts matter? Information and misinformation in American politics*. University of Oklahoma Press.

Humprecht, E. (2019). Where "Fake News" Flourishes: A Comparison across Four Western Democracies. *Information, Communication & Society, 22*(13), 1973–1988. https://doi.org/10.1080/1369118X.2018.1474241.

Humprecht, E., Castro Herrero, L., Blassnig, S., Brüggemann, M., & Engesser, S. (2022). Media Systems in the Digital Age: An Empirical Comparison of 30 Countries. *Journal of Communication, 72*(2), 145–164. https://doi.org/10.1093/joc/jqab054.

Humprecht, E., Esser, F., & Van Aelst, P. (2020). Resilience to Online Disinformation: A Framework for Cross-National Comparative Research. *The International Journal of Press/Politics*, *25*(3), 493–516. https://doi.org/10.1177/1940161219900126.

Iyengar, S., Curran, J., Lund, A. B., et al. (2010). Cross-National versus Individual-Level Differences in Political Information: A Media Systems Perspective. *Journal of Elections, Public Opinion & Parties*, *20*(3), 291–309. https://doi.org/10.1080/17457289.2010.490707.

Jastrzebski, S., & Willnat, L. (2023). Mission vs. Money: Professional Values and Attitudes of Public and Commercial Media Journalists in the United States. *Journalism Practice*, *19*(8), 1–23. https://doi.org/10.1080/17512786.2023.2282081.

Jenkins, H. (2006). *Convergence culture: Where old and new media collide*. New York University Press.

Jenssen, A. T. (2009). Does Public Broadcasting Make a Difference? Political Knowledge and Electoral Campaigns on Television. *Scandinavian Political Studies*, *32*(3), 247–271. https://doi.org/10.1111/j.1467-9477.2008.00226.x.

Jerit, J., Barabas, J., & Bolsen, T. (2006). Citizens, Knowledge, and the Information Environment. *American Journal of Political Science*, *50*(2), 266–282.

Jost, J. T., Federico, C. M., & Napier, J. L. (2009). Political Ideology: Its Structure, Functions, and Elective Affinities. *Annual Review of Psychology*, *60*(1), 307–337. https://doi.org/10.1146/annurev.psych.60.110707.163600.

Kahan, D. M. (2016). The Politically Motivated Reasoning Paradigm, Part 1: What Politically Motivated Reasoning Is and How to Measure It. In R. A. Scott & S. M. Kosslyn (Eds.), *Emerging trends in the social and behavioral sciences* (1st ed., pp. 1–16). Wiley. https://doi.org/10.1002/9781118900772.etrds0417.

Kalogeropoulos, A., & Rossini, P. (2023). Unraveling WhatsApp Group Dynamics to Understand the Threat of Misinformation in Messaging Apps. *New Media & Society27*(3), 1625–1650. https://doi.org/10.1177/14614448231199247.

Karlsen, R., Beyer, A., & Steen-Johnsen, K. (2020). Do High-Choice Media Environments Facilitate News Avoidance? A Longitudinal Study 1997–2016. *Journal of Broadcasting & Electronic Media*, *64*(5), 794–814. https://doi.org/10.1080/08838151.2020.1835428.

Kessler, G., Rizzo, S., & Kelly, M. (2020). *Donald Trump and his assault on truth: The President's falsehoods, misleading claims and flat-out lies*. Simon & Schuster.

Kocak, K., & Kıbrıs, Ö. (2023). Social Media and Press Freedom. *British Journal of Political Science*, *53*(1), 140–162. https://doi.org/10.1017/S0007123421000594.

Kovach, B., & Rosenstiel, T. (2021). *The Elements of Journalism: What Newspeople Should Know and the Public Should Expect* (4th ed., Vol. 2021). Crown.

Ksiazek, T. B., Malthouse, E. C., & Webster, J. G. (2010). News-seekers and Avoiders: Exploring Patterns of Total News Consumption across Media and the Relationship to Civic Participation. *Journal of Broadcasting & Electronic Media*, *54*(4), 551–568. https://doi.org/10.1080/08838151.2010.519808.

Kuklinski, J. H., Quirk, P. J., Jerit, J., Schwieder, D., & Rich, R. F. (2000). Misinformation and the Currency of Democratic Citizenship. *The Journal of Politics*, *62*(3), 790–816. https://doi.org/10.1111/0022-3816.00033.

Kümpel, A. S. (2020). The Matthew Effect in Social Media News Use: Assessing Inequalities in News Exposure and News Engagement on Social Network Sites (SNS). *Journalism*, *21*(8), 1083–1098. https://doi.org/10.1177/1464884920915374.

Kunda, Z. (1990). The Case for Motivated Reasoning. *Psychological Bulletin*, *108*(3), 480–498.

Lasser, J., Aroyehun, S. T., Simchon, A., et al. (2022). Social Media Sharing of Low-Quality News Sources by Political Elites. *PNAS Nexus*, *1*(4), pgac186.

Lebernegg, N., Eberl, J.-M., Tolochko, P., & Boomgaarden, H. (2024). Do You Speak Disinformation? Computational Detection of Deceptive News-Like Content Using Linguistic and Stylistic Features. *Digital Journalism*, *13*(8), 1373–1398. https://doi.org/10.1080/21670811.2024.2305792.

Lecheler, S., & Egelhofer, J. L. (2022). Disinformation, Misinformation, and Fake News: Understanding the Supply Side. In J. Strömbäck, Å. Wikforss, K. Glüer, T. Lindholm, & H. Oscarsson (Eds.), *Knowledge resistance in high-choice information environments* (pp. 69–87). Routledge.

Leeson, P. T. (2008). Media Freedom, Political Knowledge, and Participation. *Journal of Economic Perspectives*, *22*(2), 155–169. https://doi.org/10.1257/jep.22.2.155.

Leonhard, L., Karnowski, V., & Kümpel, A. S. (2020). Online and (the Feeling of Being) Informed: Online News Usage Patterns and their Relation to Subjective and Objective Political Knowledge. *Computers in Human Behavior*, *103*, 181–189. https://doi.org/10.1016/j.chb.2019.08.008.

Lind, F., & Boomgaarden, H. G. (2019). What We Do and Don't Know: A Meta-Analysis of the Knowledge Gap Hypothesis. *Annals of the International Communication Association*, *43*(3), 210–224. https://doi.org/10.1080/23808985.2019.1614475.

Lindgren, E., Damstra, A., Strömbäck, J., et al. (2022). Uninformed or Misinformed? A Review of the Conceptual-Operational Gap between

(Lack of) Knowledge and (Mis)perceptions. In J. Strömbäck, A. Wikforss, K. Glüer, T. Lindholm, & H. Oscarsson (Eds.), *Knowledge resistance in high-choice information environments* (pp. 187–206). Routledge.

Lindgren, E., Lindholm, T., Vliegenthart, R., et al. (2022). Trusting the Facts: The Role of Framing, News Media as a (Trusted) Source, and Opinion Resonance for Perceived Truth in Statistical Statements. *Journalism & Mass Communication Quarterly*, *101*(4), 981–1004. https://doi.org/10.1177/10776990221117117.

Liu, Y.-I., & Eveland, W. P. (2005). Education, Need for Cognition, and Campaign Interest as Moderators of News Effects on Political Knowledge: An Analysis of the Knowledge Gap. *Journalism & Mass Communication Quarterly*, *82*(4), 910–929. https://doi.org/10.1177/107769900508200410.

Lodge, M., & Taber, C. S. (2013). *The rationalizing voter*. Cambridge University Press.

Lupia, A. (2016). *Uninformed: Why people know so little about politics and what we can do about it*. Oxford University Press.

Maniou, T. A. (2023). The Dynamics of Influence on Press Freedom in Different Media Systems: A Comparative Study. *Journalism Practice*, *17*(9), 1937–1961. https://doi.org/10.1080/17512786.2022.2030246.

McIntyre, L. (2018). *Post-truth*. MIT Press.

Milner, H. (2002). *Civic literacy: How informed citizens make democracy work*. Tufts University Press.

Mitchell, A., Gottfried, J., Barthel, M., & Shearer, E. (2016). *The modern news consumer: News attitudes and practices in the digital era* (United States of America) [Report]. Pew Research Center. https://apo.org.au/node/65498.

Mondak, J. J., & Anderson, M. R. (2004). The Knowledge Gap: A Reexamination of Gender-Based Differences in Political Knowledge. *The Journal of Politics*, *66*(2), 492–512. https://doi.org/10.1111/j.1468-2508.2004.00161.x.

Mosleh, M., Cole, R., & Rand, D. G. (2024). Misinformation and Harmful Language Are Interconnected, Rather than Distinct, Challenges. *PNAS Nexus*, *3*(3), pgae111.

Mosleh, M., & Rand, D. G. (2022). Measuring Exposure to Misinformation from Political Elites on Twitter. *Nature Communications*, *13*(1), 7144. https://doi.org/10.1038/s41467-022-34769-6.

Mutz, D. C. (2015). *In-your-face politics: The consequences of uncivil media*. Princeton University Press. https://doi.org/10.1515/9781400865871.

Naeem, S. B., Bhatti, R., & Khan, A. (2021). An Exploration of How Fake News Is Taking over Social Media and Putting Public health at risk. *Health Information & Libraries Journal*, *38*(2), 143–149. https://doi.org/10.1111/hir.12320.

Nanz, A., & Matthes, J. (2020). Learning from Incidental Exposure to Political Information in Online Environments. *Journal of Communication, 70*(6), 769–793. https://doi.org/10.1093/joc/jqaa031.

Negroponte, N. (1995). *Being digital*. Vintage.

Newman, N., Fletcher, R., Eddy, K., Robertson, C. T., & Nielsen, R. K. (2023). *Reuters Institute Digital News Report 2023*.

Newman, N., Fletcher, R., Kalogeropoulos, A., Levy, D. A. L., & Nielsen, R. K. (2018). *Reuters institute digital news report 2018*. Reuters Institute for the Study of Journalism.

Nickerson, R. S. (1998). Confirmation Bias: A Ubiquitous Phenomenon in Many Guises. *Review of General Psychology, 2*(2), 175–220. https://doi.org/10.1037/1089-2680.2.2.175.

Nielsen, R. K., & Ganter, S. A. (2022). *The power of platforms: Shaping media and society*. Oxford University Press.

Norris, P. (2000). *A virtuous circle: Political communications in postindustrial societies*. Cambridge University Press.

Nyhan, B., Porter, E., Reifler, J., & Wood, T. J. (2020). Taking Fact-Checks Literally but not Seriously? The Effects of Journalistic Fact-Checking on Factual Beliefs and Candidate Favorability. *Political Behavior, 42*, 939–960.

Nyhan, B., & Reifler, J. (2010). When Corrections Fail: The Persistence of Political Misperceptions. *Political Behavior, 32*(2), 303–330. https://doi.org/10.1007/s11109-010-9112-2.

OECD. (2023). *PISA 2022 results (volume I): The state of learning and equity in education*. OECD. https://doi.org/10.1787/53f23881-en.

Ohme, J. (2020). Mobile but Not Mobilized? Differential Gains from Mobile News Consumption for Citizens' Political Knowledge and Campaign Participation. *Digital Journalism, 8*(1), 103–125. https://doi.org/10.1080/21670811.2019.1697625.

Ohme, J., & Mothes, C. (2020). What Affects First- and Second-Level Selective Exposure to Journalistic News? A Social Media Online Experiment. *Journalism Studies, 21*(9), 1220–1242. https://doi.org/10.1080/1461670X.2020.1735490.

Ohme, J., & Mothes, C. (2025). News Snacking and Political Learning: Changing Opportunity Structures of Digital Platform News Use and Political Knowledge. *Journal of Information Technology & Politics, 22*(1), 1–15. https://doi.org/10.1080/19331681.2023.2193579.

Önnerfors, A., & Krouwel, A. (Eds.). (2021). *Europe: Continent of conspiracies. Conspiracy theories in and about Europe*. Routledge.

Pariser, E. (2011). *The filter bubble: What the Internet is hiding from you*. Penguin UK.

Park, C. S. (2017). Do Social Media Facilitate Political Learning? Social Media Use for News, Reasoning and Political Knowledge. *The Journal of Social Media in Society*, *6*(2), 206–238.

Park, C. S., & Gil de Zúñiga, H. (2020). Learning about Politics from Mass Media and Social Media: Moderating Roles of Press Freedom and Public Service Broadcasting in 11 Countries. *International Journal of Public Opinion Research*, *33*(2), 315–335. https://doi.org/10.1093/ijpor/edaa021.

Patterson, T. E. (2013). *Informing the news: The need for knowledge-based journalism*. Vintage.

Pennycook, G., Cannon, T. D., & Rand, D. G. (2018). Prior Exposure Increases Perceived Accuracy of Fake News. *Journal of Experimental Psychology: General*, *147*(12), 1865–1880. https://doi.org/10.1037/xge0000465.

Pennycook, G., & Rand, D. G. (2019). Lazy, not Biased: Susceptibility to Partisan Fake News is Better Explained by Lack of Reasoning than by Motivated Reasoning. *Cognition*, *188*, 39–50. https://doi.org/10.1016/j.cognition.2018.06.011.

Persily, N., & Tucker, J. A. (Eds.). (2020). *Social media and democracy: The state of the field and prospects for reform*. Cambridge University Press.

Peterson, E., & Iyengar, S. (2021). Partisan Gaps in Political Information and Information-Seeking Behavior: Motivated Reasoning or Cheerleading? *American Journal of Political Science*, *65*(1), 133–147. https://doi.org/10.1111/ajps.12535.

Price, V., & Zaller, J. (1993). Who Gets the News? Alternative Measures of News Reception and their Implications for Research. *Public Opinion Quarterly*, *57*(2), 133–164. https://doi.org/10.1086/269363.

Prior, M. (2007). *Post-broadcast democracy: How media choice increases inequality in political involvement and polarizes elections*. Cambridge University Press.

Prior, M. (2019). *Hooked: How politics captures people's interest*. Cambridge University Press.

Reinemann, C., Stanyer, J., & Scherr, S. (2017). Hard and Soft News. In C. de Vreese, F. Esser, & D. N. Hopmann (Eds.), *Comparing political journalism* (pp. 131–149). Routledge.

Rekker, R. (2021). The Nature and Origins of Political Polarization Over Science. *Public Understanding of Science*, *30*(4), 352–368. https://doi.org/10.1177/0963662521989193.

Reporters without Borders. (2024). *USA: Press freedom increasingly at stake as Americans head to polls | RSF*. https://rsf.org/en/usa-press-freedom-increasingly-stake-americans-head-polls.

Rojecki, A., & Meraz, S. (2016). Rumors and Factitious Informational Blends: The Role of the Web in Speculative Politics. *New Media & Society*, *18*(1), 25–43.

Salgado, S., Strömbäck, J., Aalberg, T., & Esser, F. (2017). Interpretive Journalism. In C. de Vreese, F. Esser, & D. N. Hopmann (Eds.), *Comparing political journalism* (pp. 50–70). Routledge.

Schäfer, S. (2020). Illusion of Knowledge through Facebook News? Effects of Snack News in a News Feed on Perceived Knowledge, Attitude Strength, and Willingness for Discussions. *Computers in Human Behavior*, *103*, 1–12. https://doi.org/10.1016/j.chb.2019.08.031.

Schäfer, S., & Schemer, C. (2024). Informed Participation? An Investigation of the Relationship between Exposure to Different News Channels and Participation Mediated through Actual and Perceived Knowledge. *Frontiers in Psychology*, *14*, 1251379. https://doi.org/10.3389/fpsyg.2023.1251379.

Schoonvelde, M. (2014). Media Freedom and the Institutional Underpinnings of Political Knowledge. *Political Science Research and Methods*, *2*(2), 163–178. https://doi.org/10.1017/psrm.2013.18.

Shehata, A., Hopmann, D. N., Nord, L., & Höijer, J. (2015). Television Channel Content Profiles and Differential Knowledge Growth: A Test of the Inadvertent Learning Hypothesis Using Panel Data. *Political Communication*, *32*(3), 377–395. https://doi.org/10.1080/10584609.2014.955223.

Shehata, A., & Strömbäck, J. (2011). A Matter of Context: A Comparative Study of Media Environments and News Consumption Gaps in Europe. *Political Communication*, *28*(1), 110–134. https://doi.org/10.1080/10584609.2010.543006.

Shehata, A., & Strömbäck, J. (2021). Learning Political News from Social Media: Network Media Logic and Current Affairs News Learning in a High-Choice Media Environment. *Communication Research*, *48*(1), 125–147. https://doi.org/10.1177/0093650217749354.

Shehata, A., & Strömbäck, J. (2020). Media and Political Partisanship. In H. Oscarsson & S. Holmberg (Eds.), *Research handbook on political partisanship* (pp. 60–73). Edward Elgar.

Shin, J., & Thorson, K. (2017). Partisan Selective Sharing: The Biased Diffusion of Fact-Checking Messages on Social Media: Sharing Fact-Checking Messages on Social Media. *Journal of Communication*, *67*(2), 233–255. https://doi.org/10.1111/jcom.12284.

Shoemaker, P. J., & Vos, T. P. (2009). *Gatekeeping theory*. Routledge.

Skovsgaard, M., & Andersen, K. (2020). Conceptualizing News Avoidance: Towards a Shared Understanding of Different Causes and Potential Solutions.

Journalism Studies, *21*(4), 459–476. https://doi.org/10.1080/1461670X.2019.1686410.

Skovsgaard, M., Shehata, A., & Strömbäck, J. (2016). Opportunity Structures for Selective Exposure: Investigating Selective Exposure and Learning in Swedish Election Campaigns Using Panel Survey Data. *The International Journal of Press/Politics*, *21*(4), 527–546. https://doi.org/10.1177/1940161216658157.

Soroka, S. (2014). *Negativity in democratic politics: Causes and consequences*. Cambridge University Press.

Soroka, S., Andrew, B., Aalberg, T., et al. (2013). Auntie Knows Best? Public Broadcasters and Current Affairs Knowledge. *British Journal of Political Science*, *43*(4), 719–739. https://doi.org/10.1017/S0007123412000555.

StataCorp. (2021). *Stata statistical software: Release 17* [Computer software]. StataCorp.

Stępińska, A., Adamczewska, K., Secler, B., et al. (In press). Between Citizens, Business, and Political Parties: How Polish Journalists Perform their Professional Roles under Contradictory Pressures. In C. Mellado (Ed.), *Journalistic roles and news content: Global perspectives*. Peter Lang.

Stępnik, K. (2023). Lex TVN. Przebieg debaty publicznej. *Przegląd Sejmowy*, *4 (177)*, 119–150. https://doi.org/10.31268/PS.2023.200.

Štětka, V., & Mihelj, S. (2024). *The illiberal public sphere: Media in polarized societies*. Springer Nature Switzerland. https://doi.org/10.1007/978-3-031-54489-7.

Strömbäck, J. (2017). Does Public Service TV and the Intensity of the Political Information Environment Matter? *Journalism Studies*, *18*(11), 1415–1432. https://doi.org/10.1080/1461670X.2015.1133253.

Strömbäck, J., Boomgaarden, H., Broda, E., et al. (2022). From Low-Choice to High-Choice Media Environments: Implications for Knowledge Resistance. In J. Strömbäck, A. Wikforss, K. Glüer, T. Lindholm, T., & H. Oscarsson. (Eds.), *Knowledge resistance in high-choice information environments* (pp. 49–68). Routledge.

Strömbäck, J., Djerf-Pierre, M., & Shehata, A. (2013). The Dynamics of Political Interest and News Media Consumption: A Longitudinal Perspective. *International Journal of Public Opinion Research*, *25*(4), 414–435. https://doi.org/10.1093/ijpor/eds018.

Strömbäck, J., Lindgren, E., Tsfati, Y., et al. (2023). Political Opinion Leaders in High-Choice Information Environments: Are They More Informed Than Others? *Mass Communication and Society*, *27*(5), 949–971. https://doi.org/10.1080/15205436.2023.2281311.

Strömbäck, J., Tsfati, Y., Boomgaarden, H., et al. (2020). News Media Trust and Its Impact on Media Use: Toward a Framework for Future Research. *Annals of the International Communication Association*, *44*(2), 139–156. https://doi.org/10.1080/23808985.2020.1755338.

Strömbäck, J., Wikforss, Å., Glüer, K., Lindholm, T., & Oscarsson, H. (2022). *Knowledge resistance in high-choice information environments*. Routledge.

Stroud, N. J., Peacock, C., & Curry, A. L. (2020). The Effects of Mobile Push Notifications on News Consumption and Learning. *Digital Journalism*, *8*(1), 32–48. https://doi.org/10.1080/21670811.2019.1655462.

Szostek, J. (2018a). News Media Repertoires and Strategic Narrative Reception: A Paradox of Dis/belief in Authoritarian Russia. *New Media & Society*, *20*(1), 68–87. https://doi.org/10.1177/1461444816656638.

Szostek, J. (2018b). Nothing Is True? The Credibility of News and Conflicting Narratives during "Information War" in Ukraine. *The International Journal of Press/Politics*, *23*(1), 116–135. https://doi.org/10.1177/1940161217743258.

Theocharis, Y., Cardenal, A., Jin, S., et al. (2023). Does the Platform Matter? Social Media and COVID-19 Conspiracy Theory Beliefs in 17 Countries. *New Media & Society*, *25*(12), 3412–3437. https://doi.org/10.1177/14614448211045666.

Thorson, E. A. (2024a). *How news coverage of misinformation shapes perceptions and trust*. Cambridge University Press. https://doi.org/10.1017/9781009488815.

Thorson, E. A. (2024b). *The invented state: Policy misperceptions in the American public*. Oxford University Press.

Tichenor, P. J., Donohue, G. A., & Olien, C. N. (1970). Mass Media Flow and Differential Growth in Knowledge. *Public Opinion Quarterly*, *34*(2), 159. https://doi.org/10.1086/267786.

Toff, B., & Kalogeropoulos, A. (2020). All the News That's Fit to Ignore. *Public Opinion Quarterly*, *84*(S1), 366–390. https://doi.org/10.1093/poq/nfaa016.

Toff, B., Palmer, R., & Nielsen, R. K. (2024). *Avoiding the news: Reluctant audiences for journalism*. Columbia University Press.

Tsfati, Y., Boomgaarden, H. G., Strömbäck, J., et al. (2020). Causes and consequences of mainstream media dissemination of fake news: Literature review and synthesis. *Annals of the International Communication Association*, *44*(2), 157–173. https://doi.org/10.1080/23808985.2020.1759443.

Uscinski, J. E., & Parent, J. M. (2014). *American conspiracy theories*. Oxford University Press.

Usher, N. (2021). *News for the rich, white, and blue: How place and power distort American journalism*. Columbia University Press.

Vaccari, C., Chadwick, A., & Kaiser, J. (2023). The Campaign Disinformation Divide: Believing and Sharing News in the 2019 UK General Election. *Political Communication*, *40*(1), 4–23. https://doi.org/10.1080/10584609.2022.2128948.

Valenzuela, S., Bachmann, I., & Bargsted, M. (2023). The Personal Is the Political? What Do Whatsapp Users Share and How It Matters for News Knowledge, Polarization and Participation in Chile. In E. Mitchelstein & P. J. Boczkowski (Eds.), *Digital journalism in Latin America* (pp. 26–46). Routledge.

Van Aelst, P., Strömbäck, J., Aalberg, T., et al. (2017). Political Communication in a High-Choice Media Environment: A Challenge for Democracy? *Annals of the International Communication Association*, *41*(1), 3–27. https://doi.org/10.1080/23808985.2017.1288551.

Van Aelst, P., Van Erkel, P., Castro, L., et al. (2025). The Limits of Social Media as a Source of Political Information during Routine and Crisis Times across 17 Countries. *Journal of Information Technology & Politics*, 1–17. https://doi.org/10.1080/19331681.2025.2501033.

van der Linden, W. J., & Hambleton, R. K. (1997). *Handbook of modern item response theory*. Springer.

van der Meer, T. W. G., Walter, A., & Van Aelst, P. (2016). The Contingency of Voter Learning: How Election Debates Influenced Voters' Ability and Accuracy to Position Parties in the 2010 Dutch Election Campaign. *Political Communication*, *33*(1), 136–157. https://doi.org/10.1080/10584609.2015.1016639.

van Erkel, P. F. A., & Van Aelst, P. (2021). Why Don't We Learn from Social Media? Studying Effects of and Mechanisms behind Social Media News Use on General Surveillance Political Knowledge. *Political Communication*, *38*(4), 407–425. https://doi.org/10.1080/10584609.2020.1784328.

Vermeer, S. A. M., Kruikemeier, S., Trilling, D., & de Vreese, C. H. (2021). WhatsApp with Politics?! Examining the Effects of Interpersonal Political Discussion in Instant Messaging Apps. *The International Journal of Press/Politics*, *26*(2), 410–437. https://doi.org/10.1177/1940161220925020.

Villi, M., Aharoni, T., Tenenboim-Weinblatt, K., et al. (2022). Taking a Break from News: A Five-Nation Study of News Avoidance in the Digital Era. *Digital Journalism*, *10*(1), 148–164. https://doi.org/10.1080/21670811.2021.1904266.

Vliegenthart, R., Stromback, J., Boomgaarden, H., et al. (2023). Taking Political Alternative Media into Account: Investigating the Linkage between Media Repertoires and (Mis)perceptions. *Mass Communication and Society*, *27*(5), 877–901. https://doi.org/10.1080/15205436.2023.2251444.

Walter, N., Brooks, J. J., Saucier, C. J., & Suresh, S. (2020). Evaluating the Impact of Attempts to Correct Health Misinformation on Social Media: A Meta-Analysis. *Health Communication*, *36*(13), 1776–1784. https://doi.org/10.1080/10410236.2020.1794553.

Weeks, B. E. (2024). *Angry and wrong: The emotional dynamics of partisan media and political misperceptions*. Cambridge University Press.

Wojcieszak, M., Casas, A., Yu, X., Nagler, J., & Tucker, J. A. (2022). Most Users Do Not Follow Political Elites on Twitter; those Who Do Show Overwhelming Preferences for Ideological Congruity. *Science Advances*, *8*(39), eabn9418. https://doi.org/10.1126/sciadv.abn9418.

Yamamoto, M., Kushin, M. J., & Dalisay, F. (2018). How Informed Are Messaging App Users about Politics? A Linkage of Messaging App Use and Political Knowledge and Participation. *Telematics and Informatics*, *35*(8), 2376–2386. https://doi.org/10.1016/j.tele.2018.10.008.

Young, D. G. (2023). *Wrong. How media, politics, and identity drive our appetite for misinformation*. John Hopkins University Press.

Zaller, J. (2003). A New Standard of News Quality: Burglar Alarms for the Monitorial Citizen. *Political Communication*, *20*(2), 109–130. https://doi.org/10.1080/10584600390211136.

Zhao, X., & Bleske, G. L. (1998). Horse-Race Polls and Audience Issue Learning. *Harvard International Journal of Press/Politics*, *3*(4), 13–34. https://doi.org/10.1177/1081180X98003004004.

Zilinsky, J., Theocharis, Y., Pradel, F., et al. (2024). Justifying an Invasion: When Is Disinformation Successful? *Political Communication*, *41*(6), 965–986. https://doi.org/10.1080/10584609.2024.2352483.

Zoizner, A., Sheafer, T., Castro, L., et al. (2022). The Effects of the COVID-19 Outbreak on Selective Exposure: Evidence from 17 Countries. *Political Communication*, *39*(5), 674–696. https://doi.org/10.1080/10584609.2022.2107745.

Funding Statement

This project lead by David N. Hopmann as the principal investigator (file number 462.19.449) is financially supported by the NORFACE Joint Research Programme on Democratic Governance in a Turbulent Age and co-funded by FWO, DFF, ANR, DFG, NWO, NCN, AEI, and ESRC, and the European Commission through Horizon 2020 under grant agreement number 822166.

Cambridge Elements

Politics and Communication

Stuart Soroka
University of California, Los Angeles

Stuart Soroka is a Professor in the Departments of Communication and Political Science at the University of California, Los Angeles. His research focuses on political communication, political psychology, and the relationships between public policy, public opinion and mass media. His books with Cambridge University Press include *Information and Democracy* (2022, with Christopher Wlezien), *The Increasing Viability of Good News* (2021, with Yanna Krupnikov), *Negativity in Democratic Politics* (2014), and *Degrees of Democracy* (2010, with Christopher Wlezien).

About the Series

Cambridge Elements in Politics and Communication publishes research focused on the intersection of media, technology, and politics. The series emphasizes forward-looking reviews of the field, path-breaking theoretical and methodological innovations, and the timely application of social-scientific theory and methods to current developments in politics and communication around the world.

Cambridge Elements

Politics and Communication

Elements in the Series

The Increasing Viability of Good News
Stuart Soroka and Yanna Krupnikov

Digital Transformations of the Public Arena
Andreas Jungherr and Ralph Schroeder

Battleground: Asymmetric Communication Ecologies and the Erosion of Civil Society in Wisconsin
Lewis A. Friedland, Dhavan V. Shah, Michael W. Wagner, Katherine J. Cramer, Chris Wells, and Jon Pevehouse

Constructing Political Expertise in the News
Kathleen Searles, Yanna Krupnikov, John Barry Ryan, and Hillary Style

The YouTube Apparatus
Kevin Munger

How News Coverage of Misinformation Shapes Perceptions and Trust
Emily Thorson

Angry and Wrong: The Emotional Dynamics of Partisan Media and Political Misperceptions
Brian E. Weeks

Social Media Democracy Mirage: How Social Media News Fuels a Politically Uninformed Participatory Democracy
Homero Gil de Zúñiga, Hugo Marcos-Marne, Manuel Goyanes, and Rebecca Scheffauer

Political Representation as Communicative Practice
Fabio Wolkenstein and Christopher Wratil

Amplifying Extremism: Small Town Politicians, Media Storms, and American Journalism
Nik Usher and Jessica C. Hagman

Catching Fire in the News: The Necessary Conditions for Media Storms
Amber E. Boydstun, Jill R. Laufer, Dallas Card, and Noah A. Smith

News Use, Political Knowledge, and Misperceptions in 18 Countries across the Global North
Peter Van Aelst, Luisa Gehle, Christian Schemer, Jesper Strömbäck, and Alon Zoizner

A full series listing is available at: www.cambridge.org/EPCM

For EU product safety concerns, contact us at Calle de José Abascal, 56–1º,
28003 Madrid, Spain or eugpsr@cambridge.org.